Culturally Relevant Teaching

Culturally Relevant Teaching

Preparing Teachers to Include All Learners

Edited by Megan Adams, Sanjuana Rodriguez, and Kate Zimmer

ROWMAN & LITTLEFIELD
Lanham • Boulder • New York • London

Published by Rowman & Littlefield
A wholly owned subsidiary of The Rowman & Littlefield Publishing Group, Inc.
4501 Forbes Boulevard, Suite 200, Lanham, Maryland 20706
www.rowman.com

Unit A, Whitacre Mews, 26-34 Stannary Street, London SE11 4AB

British Library Cataloguing in Publication Information Available

Library of Congress Cataloging-in-Publication Data Available

ISBN 978-1-4758-3478-9 (cloth : alk. paper)
ISBN 978-1-4758-3479-6 (pbk. : alk. paper)
ISBN 978-1-4758-3480-2 (electronic)

♾ ™ The paper used in this publication meets the minimum requirements of American National Standard for Information Sciences Permanence of Paper for Printed Library Materials, ANSI/NISO Z39.48-1992.

Printed in the United States of America

For AJ, with all my love.
—MGA

Para Samuel, con todo el amor del mundo.
—SCR

To my boys—thank you for making each day brighter. Love you
bunches.
—KZ

Contents

Preface

Megan Adams, Kate Zimmer, and Sanjuana Rodriguez

CULTURALLY RELEVANT PEDAGOGY IN OUR FIELDS

The common thread in this edited volume is inclusivity of all students. Across the authors' fields of education, there are a variety of ways inclusion occurs. The chapters in this text provide examples of research and practice that will help teachers in their quest to foster literacy success in all learners.

In some chapters, authors question their use of culturally relevant pedagogy and reflect on the use of deficit language by themselves and others in education (Bartolome, 1994; Ladson-Billings, 1995a, 1995b, 1998). In other chapters, authors present studies that focus on assisting families, students, teachers, and researchers become more inclusive in their practices and beliefs. Finally, several chapters describe studies that investigate and showcase culturally relevant pedagogy in practice.

Culturally relevant pedagogy (CRP) spans disciplines, yet often practitioners are blind to practices that hinder its progress (Ladson-Billings, 1995a). For example, students who perform below grade level are often diagnosed and characterized with deficit-based language, thus impeding the mere construct of CRP (Iannacci and Graham, 2013). The purpose of this volume is to describe inclusive practices that promote the success of all students.

CULTURALLY RELEVANT PEDAGOGY IN LITERACY EDUCATION

Paolo Freire argues in *Pedagogy of the Oppressed* (1970) that all people, no matter the extent to which their voices have been silenced by the oppressors in their culture, are able to think and speak critically about the world. The key to their liberation, he argues, is literacy. For that reason, Freire is frequently cited in literacy studies investigating culturally relevant pedagogy (Camangian, 2010; Larrotta and Yamamura, 2011).

Freire's work is also frequently cited in studies of "new literacies" (Lankshear and Knobel, 2013; Lankshear and Knobel, 2003; New London Group, 1996). The field of new literacies encompasses more than digital literacies; scholars in the field often study how to incorporate inclusive literacy practices that are a better reflection of the diverse cultures of P–12 students (Lankshear and Knobel, 2003; New London Group, 1996).

This text incorporates new approaches in literacy education to meet the needs of all students. In addition, as literacy educators who study the field of new literacies—many of us prefer the multiple literacies terminology used by the New London Group (1996)—the aim of this text is to provide snapshots of practices and research that foster the literacy development of all children.

In literacy education, this often means providing information about diagnostic assessments and interventions through asset-based language, using a strength-based approach to describe assessment results for children performing below grade level in reading. These chapters highlight the efforts made by teachers, preservice teachers, and researchers to learn and incorporate asset-based models in their classrooms, schools, and courses.

CULTURALLY RELEVANT PEDAGOGY IN INCLUSIVE EDUCATION

The field of special education has brought the concept of including all students to the mainstream through the broader term of "inclusive education"; therefore, it is important to understand the construct of inclusion (Danforth and Naraian, 2015; Kozleski, Yu, and Satter, 2015; Nasibullov, Kashapova, and Shavallyeva, 2015). In the context of this book—and the lens through which we conduct our research, teach, and write—the term "inclusive education" refers to teaching that addresses the needs of all students.

This shift addresses a call to action by many researchers to avoid making generalizations about students based on their disabilities (Connor and Ferri, 2005; Ferri, Gallagher, and Connor, 2011; Sleeter, 1986). Critical disability theory assists us as editors to avoid using "diversity" and "inclusion" synonymously (Ferri, Gallagher, and Connor, 2011). In this text, the term "diverse students" represents students who are culturally and linguistically diverse; describing "reaching all students" includes diverse students and students with exceptionalities.

Defining the terms "inclusive" and "diverse students" is important in framing the articles in this volume, which is based on the knowledge that students of color are overrepresented in special education. Studies have shown that placement can be used to further marginalize students of color in particular (Connor and Ferri, 2005; Ferri, Gallagher, and Connor, 2011; Harris et al., 2004; Jordan, 2005).

PREPARING TEACHERS TO WORK WITH ALL LEARNERS

As researchers and former classroom teachers, we often hear and observe educators struggle with how to effectively instruct all students in the area of literacy. Despite the recent emphasis on preparing teachers to work with all learners, more must be done to ensure that all students have equitable access to the general curriculum (Brown et al., 2008; García and Tyler, 2010; McHatton and Parker, 2013).

Many districts we work with list students' reading performance as a top concern. With funding cuts, there are fewer instructional coaches, graduation coaches, and literacy coaches to implement the needed professional development to prepare teachers to reach children performing across reading levels.

OPPORTUNITY GAP AS IT APPLIES TO ALL STUDENTS

Too often, we have seen reading programs fail because the program was implemented without support and appropriate reading expertise. Further complicating matters, the literacy needs of elementary schools are complex. There are issues specifically related to the growing demand for young students to develop strong literacy skills; there are also sociocultural issues that contribute to the success of students. These needs, coupled with new educational policies that mandate new programs and assessments, create a unique challenge for elementary schools.

One of the most pressing issues is the continued achievement gap, often referred to as the "opportunity gap" (Boykin and Noguera, 2011), for diverse students. This gap between the academic performance of African American students and Latino/a students compared to that of white students has been widely documented (Getzel and Thoma, 2008; Jencks and Phillips, 2011; McHatton and McCray, 2007).

When looking at any "subgroup" in educational data, there is a tendency to generalize and simplify the varied identities of students. We argue that structures in place in schools continue to keep students from achieving equally; we therefore prefer the term "opportunity gap," rather than "achievement gap," to describe the failure of schools to equitably provide access for all learners.

Research continues to chronicle that schools do not provide the necessary exposure to literacy practices that benefit all students. This lack of opportunity equates to a lack of evidence-based, differentiated literacy practices across P–12 classrooms for all students; those practices provide access to "academic and social ways" that promote success in school (Paris, 2012, p. 94).

Therefore, diverse students and students with exceptionalities are labeled as deficient, and they have limited access to the literacy skills necessary for them to become proficient readers and to make adequately yearly progress as measured by standardized tests (Justice and Ezell, 2001; Massetti, 2009; Whitehurst and Lonigan, 1998). The tendency to follow the data in educational reports and work on addressing the "needs of" subgroups further marginalizes students (Paris, 2012).

THE PURPOSE OF THIS BOOK

Throughout our collective experiences we have heard the following statements:

"I'm a high school teacher! I wasn't trained to teach reading!"
"We are staffing a reading lab and need more ELA certified teachers."
"I can't teach word problems to a child who cannot read at grade level!"
"How can a child learn science concepts with no vocabulary comprehension?"
"I don't know how to teach students with disabilities."

These cries for help and voices of frustration are why we set out to write this book—to share practical and evidence-based strategies that enable teachers to build an inclusive, literacy-rich environment where all students feel confident, supported, and successful.

This volume spans the P–12 spectrum and includes chapters on the literacy of students with disabilities, culturally relevant pedagogy, literacy and bilingual students, literacy in elementary mathematics, teachers' perceptions of culturally relevant literacy instruction, literacy and gifted students, and bridging the literacy gap through a summer bridge program.

The strategies in this book are based on our own experiences and research as educators. All of these chapters focus on strategies teachers and schools might use to improve their students' literacy. We pose the question: How can we work together as communities to improve the literacy performance of all students?

The following chapters describe practices that allow teachers to begin the process of including all students, to develop their inclusive practices, and to reflect on inclusive practices they already use in their classrooms and schools. Together the authors stress the importance of providing access to the general education curriculum to *all* students.

REFERENCES

Bartolome, L. (1994). Beyond the methods fetish: Toward a humanizing pedagogy. *Harvard Educational Review*, 64(2), 173–95.

Boykin, A. W., and Noguera, P. (2011). *Creating the opportunity to learn: Moving from research to practice to close the achievement gap*. Alexandria, VA: Association for Supervision and Curriculum Development.

Brown, K. S., Welsh, L. A., Hill, K. H., and Cipko, J. P. (2008). The efficacy of embedding special education instruction in teacher preparation programs in the United States. *Teaching and Teacher Education*, 24, 2087–94.

Camangian, P. (2010). Starting with self: Teaching autoethnography to foster critically caring literacies. *Research in the Teaching of English*, 45(2), 179–204.

Connor, D. J., and Ferri, B. A. (2005). Integration and inclusion: A troubling nexus; Race, disability, and special education. *Journal of African American History*, 90(1/2), 107–27.

Danforth, S., and Naraian, S. (2015). This new field of inclusive education: Beginning a dialogue on conceptual foundations. *Intellectual and Developmental Disabilities*, 53(1), 70–85.

Ferri, B. A., Gallagher, D., and Connor, D. J. (2011). Pluralizing methodologies in the field of LD: From "what works" to what matters. *Learning Disability Quarterly*, 34(3), 222–31.

Freire, P. (1970). *Pedagogy of the oppressed*. New York: Herder and Herder.

García, S., and Tyler, B. J. (2010). Meeting the needs of English language learners with learning disabilities in the general curriculum. *Theory into Practice*, 49(2), 113–20.

Getzel, E. E., and Thoma, C. A. (2008). Experiences of college students with disabilities and the importance of self-determination in higher education settings. *Career Development for Exceptional Individuals*, 31(2), 77–84.

Harris, J. J., Brown, E. L., Ford, D. Y., and Richardson, J. W. (2004). African Americans and multicultural education: A proposed remedy for disproportionate special education and underinclusion in gifted education. *Education and Urban Society*, 36(3), 304–41.

Iannacci, L., and Graham, B. (2013). Reconceptualizing "special education" curriculum in a bachelor of education program: Teacher candidates discourse and teacher education practices. *Canadian Journal of Disability Studies*, 2(2), 10–34.

Jencks, C., and Phillips, M. (Eds.). (2011). *The black-white test score gap*. Washington, DC: Brookings Institution Press.

Jordan, K. (2005). Discourses of difference and the overrepresentation of black students in special education. *Journal of African American History*, 90(1/2), 128–49.

Justice, L. M. and Ezell, H. K. (2001). Written language awareness in preschool children from low-income households: A descriptive analysis. *Communication Disorders Quarterly*, 22(3), 123-134

Justice, L. M., and Kaderavek, J. N. (2002). Using shared storybook reading to promote emergent literacy. *Council for Exceptional Children*, 34, 8–13.

Kozleski, E. B., Yu, T., and Satter, A. L. (2015). A never ending journey: Inclusive education is a principle of practice, not an end game. *Research and Practice for Persons with Severe Disabilities*, 40(3), 211–26.

Ladson-Billings, G. (1995a). But that's just good teaching! The case for culturally relevant pedagogy. *Theory into Practice*, 34(3), 159–66.

Ladson-Billings, G. (1995b). Toward a theory of culturally relevant pedagogy. *American Educational Research Journal*, 32(3), 455–61.

Ladson-Billings, G. (1998). Just what is critical race theory and what's it doing in a nice field like education? *International Journal of Qualitative Studies in Education*, 11(1), 7–24.

Lankshear, C., and Knobel, M. (2003). *New literacies: Changing knowledge and classroom learning.* Philadelphia, PA: Open University Press.

Lankshear, C., and Knobel, M. (Eds.) (2013). *A new literacies reader.* New York: Peter Lang.

Larrotta, C., and Yamamura, E. K. (2011). A community cultural wealth approach to Latina/ Latino parent involvement: The promise of family literacy. *Adult Basic Education and Literacy Journal*, 5(2), 74–83.

Massetti, G. M. (2009). Enhancing emergent literacy skills of preschoolers from low-income environments through a classroom-based approach. *School Psychology*, 4, 554–69.

McHatton, P. A., and McCray, E. D. (2007). Inclination toward inclusion: Perceptions of elementary and secondary education teacher candidates. *Action in Teacher Education*, 29(3), 25–32.

McHatton, P. A., and Parker, A. (2013). Purposeful preparation: Longitudinally exploring inclusion attitudes of general and special education pre-service teachers. *Journal of the Teacher Education Division of the Council for Exceptional Children*, 36, 186–203.

Nasibullov, R. R., Kashapova, L. M., and Shavallyeva, Z. S. (2015). Conditions of formation of social successfulness of students with disabilities in the system of continuous inclusive education on the basis of value approach. *International Journal of Environmental and Science Education*, 10(4), 543–52.

New London Group. (1996). A pedagogy of multiliteracies: Designing social futures. *Harvard Educational Review*, 66, 60–92.

Paris, D. (2012). Culturally sustaining pedagogy a needed change in stance, terminology, and practice. *Educational Researcher*, 41(3), 93–97.

Sleeter, C. E. (1986). Learning disabilities: The social construction of a special education category. *Exceptional Children*, 53(1), 46-54.

Whitehurst, G. J., and Lonigan, C. J. (1998). Child development and emergent literacy. *Child Development*, 69(3), 848–72.

I

Culturally Relevant Pedagogy and Students with Exceptionalities

Chapter One

Enhancing Social Development for Preschool Students with Autism

A Teacher's Guide

Kate Zimmer

Introduction Classroom Example: Mrs. Card and Ryan

Mrs. Card's four-year-old preschool classroom is an exciting place to be. Beyond the child-sized chairs, kid furniture, and rug for circle time, her classroom is filled with opportunities that encourage interactive learning activities. The classroom is decorated to reflect this month's theme, "The Great Outdoors." There's a green child-sized tent in the dramatic play center. In the reading corner, there are children's storybooks about animals and insects, and plastic ants fill the sand tub center.

Mrs. Card smiles as she looks around her classroom and sees how engaged her students are; they are really enjoying this month's theme! But one little boy, Ryan, sits all alone at the reading corner. Ryan's parents informed Mrs. Card at the beginning of the year that Ryan has autism. Although Mrs. Card is familiar with autism and understands that Ryan will have more difficulty communicating and interacting socially with his peers, she can't help but wonder how to encourage him to play with others in the class.

WHY STUDENTS WITH AUTISM HAVE SOCIAL AND LANGUAGE PROBLEMS

According to the Centers for Disease Control Prevention (2014), an average of one in sixty-eight children has an autism spectrum disorder (ASD), a number that has increased tremendously in the last decade. Autism is commonly defined as a neurodevelopmental disorder characterized by impairments in an individual's social and communicative development, which is often accompanied by stereotyped patterns of behavior and/or interest (American Psychological Association, 2014). Experts describe autism as a spectrum disorder because of the broad set of characteristics and functional skills individuals display (Jones and Feeley, 2007; Leach and LaRocque, 2011).

Autism and Language Issues

Language delays and social impairment are two of the hallmark features for children who have ASD. Children on the spectrum may show difficulty using spoken language, understanding and using gestures, an inability to imitate others, and a hard time with appropriate conversation with their family members and peers. These difficulties in communication and social skills are among the most common reasons for initial referrals for young children with autism (Thurm et al., 2007).

Because of difficultly with language and social skills, some children with autism become frustrated and exhibit behavioral problems at home and in the classroom. These social outbursts can cause isolation from peers, making it difficult for children with ASD to develop appropriate peer relationships. Young children with ASD also have great difficulty understanding the spoken word, especially emotional words. This is because words such as *love, joy,* and *anger* are abstract; that is, they refer to ideas or concepts without any physical references to figure out the meaning of the word through context. As a result, children with ASD need to be taught these abstract words through visual concepts like pictures and objects.

The Role of Joint Attention

Not only do children on the spectrum have language delays, they also have notable difficulties with joint attention (Isaken and Holth, 2009). Bruner's (1978) research has demonstrated that young children use joint attention to help them comprehend the world around them. It plays a pivotal role in acquiring language, from gaining knowledge of new words to understanding

Table 1.1.   Examples of Abstract Words

adventure	beauty	confused
death	envy	friendship
generous	happiness	hate
intelligence	kindness	love
luck	need	peace

the events happening in the child's environment. A deficit in joint attention is one of the earliest and most common signs of autism.

Joint attention, described as two persons sharing attention on the same external object through the use of gaze or gestures, is considered a fundamental milestone in part because it contributes to children learning object labels, thus enabling them to make sense of language around them (Jones and Carr, 2004; Murray et al., 2008; Vismara and Lyons, 2007).

Children with ASD have significantly more difficulty following head turns, eye gaze, and pointing than typically developing children (Jones and Carr, 2004; Jones and Feeley, 2007). Numerous studies of joint attention and language development of children with autism support the idea that important indicators of language occur prior to verbalizations. For example, children's preverbal ability to coordinate their attention between an object and a person ultimately allows them to understand the expressions and gestures being used by others (Mundy, Sigman, and Kasari, 1990; Murray et al., 2008; Vismara and Lyons, 2007).

Additional research concludes that specific language deficits that characterize autism are developmentally related to the failure of joint attention mechanics in infancy and early childhood. As a result of the impairment of joint attention that children with autism display, the syntax and semantics of language usually acquired during this stage of development are repressed (Loveland and Landry, 1986). Therefore, the strategies and techniques that

Figure 1.1.   The teacher and boy have joint attention on the truck. Kate Zimmer

are required to use the pragmatics of language effectively need to be explicitly taught in the classroom.

How Joint Attention and Emergent Literacy Relate

Early childhood educators need to actively engage children in literacy opportunities, activities, and experiences (Shedd and Duke, 2008). Ideally, preschool literacy experiences should be integrated throughout the day, throughout the curriculum, and in the home environment (Johnston, McDonnell, and Hawken, 2008). Exposing preschool-aged children to print through interactions with adults provides them a variety of opportunities to communicate via literacy, which can benefit all children, regardless of socioeconomic status, ethnicity, disability, or ability level (Fielding-Barnsley and Purdie, 2003; Justice and Ezell, 2002; Beauchat, Blamey, and Walpole, 2009; Lane and Wright, 2007).

The emergent literacy knowledge and skills received from preschool strongly correlate with later academic performance. For children in preschool to acquire these skills, activities must focus on phonological awareness, print awareness, letter recognition, and early writing (Johnston, McDonnell, and Hawken, 2008).

These important literacy experiences become complex for practitioners when their preschool students with ASD have deficits in joint attention. This is because joint attention is a prerequisite for acquiring emergent literacy skills. Therefore, it is vital for early educators to work on increasing joint attention with these children throughout the school day.

Current research suggests that instruction centered on literacy objectives increases children's oral language, demonstrating the critical role educators have in creating meaningful opportunities to work on these joint attention skills (Lanter and Waston, 2008). Once children with ASD display joint attention, they have the essential skill needed to acquire the literacy skills desirable for future academic success.

WHAT TEACHERS CAN DO TO INCREASE SOCIAL DEVELOPMENT IN THEIR CLASSROOMS

The following strategies can be easily implemented by teachers to enhance social development for children on the spectrum throughout the school day. All strategies are evidenced-based and could lay the groundwork for literacy gains.

Setting the Environment

Setting up the preschool classroom environment to support natural joint attention exchanges is important. When interactions are allowed to flow freely in day-to-day classroom activities, children with autism are less stressed and tend to be more relaxed. Teachers can then look beyond preplanned activities and incorporate natural learning opportunities for skill development (Pierce, Munier, and Myers, 2009). Center time, although structured, follows a more naturalistic behavioral plan, providing teachers numerous opportunities to increase joint attention with their ASD students (Isaksen and Holth, 2009; Vismara and Lyons, 2007).

Here are a few tips for setting the classroom environment:

- Position yourself to create face-to-face interactions with the student. Holding activities and materials at the child's eye level will increase the opportunity for interaction (Johnston, McDonnell, and Hawken, 2008; Justice and Kaderavek, 2002).
- Follow the student's lead to boost natural engagement. For example, if a child points to a bear, provide the child with specific and descriptive feedback, such as "You are pointing to a big brown bear. See him smiling. The bear is smiling because he is happy" (Lane and Wright, 2007; Lanter and Watson, 2008; Justice and Pullen, 2003).
- Identify materials and objects that are interesting to the student and place them in and around your center areas. While using the child's restrictive

Table 1.2. Strategies at a Glance

Strategy	Description
Setting the Environment	Create a classroom that supports natural exchanges: face-to-face interactions, materials at child's level, follow child's lead, use objects of child's interest, and use expression and inflection when communicating.
Wait Time	After asking a question, wait three to five seconds to allow the child to process and answer the question. In addition, use embellished gestures and/or body language to indicate to the child that a response is expected.
Adult/Peer Imitation	Instruction using a "Simon Says" format is a way for a child with autism to practice and master a new skill.
Playful Block	Purposefully and playfully get in the way of an object the child wants.
Playful Arrangement	Using this method, a teacher turns the experience of a child playing alone into an opportunity for social engagement.
Playful Negotiation	This method enables a teacher to extend or stretch out an interaction as much possible.

interest to your benefit, make certain that these materials are developmentally appropriate for the child (Justice and Kaderavek, 2002; Roberts, Jurgens, and Burchinal, 2005).

- Use lots of expression and inflection in your voice. Exaggerating your voice and facial expressions will help children focus on you and keep them interested in the interaction. Voice inflections and facial expressions will also help them understand the meaning behind abstract and emotional words (Johnston, McDonnell, and Hawken, 2008; Lane and Wright, 2007).

A Classroom Example of Setting the Environment

> *Mrs. Card sees Ryan, a four-year-old student with autism, sitting in the reading center. He is flipping through* The Icky Bug Alphabet Book. *Mrs. Card purposely places books about insects into the reading center because Ryan has a deep interest in bugs and other crawly creatures. Mrs. Card sees center time as a perfect opportunity to practice some joint attention skills with the little boy.*
>
> *She carefully positions herself in front of Ryan, taps on the book to get his attention, and says, "That looks like a great book about bugs." The child looks at the teacher and points to a bug on the page, establishing joint attention. Mrs. Card smiles and says, "Ryan, you pointed to a red ladybug, wonderful job! Please point to the green frog on the page."*
>
> *Ryan then points to the green frog on the page and looks up at Mrs. Card, again responding to her bid for joint attention. Mrs. Card smiles big and says, "Great job, Ryan! You pointed to the green frog."*

Wait Time

As teachers, on average we wait less than one second for a child to respond to us before we answer for them or ask another child to respond (Rowe, 1986)! It is important to give all children, autistic or not, time to process questions and respond. Using a wait time of three to five seconds is a natural and easy way to increase the number of opportunities children have to communicate with their environment (Hughes and Fredrick, 2006).

If teachers do not wait three to five seconds for a child to respond, they might be missing an important communication attempt by the child. Using a delay strategy also cues preschool students that a response is wanted (Mirenda and Iacono, 1988). Here are a few "wait time" tips:

- Use a brief pause of three to five seconds accompanied by an expectant look. Use embellished gestures and body language to indicate that a response is expected (Hughes and Fredrick, 2006; Justice and Kaderavek, 2002; Lane and Wright, 2007; Mirenda and Iacono, 1988).

- Keep pauses between three and five seconds (Hughes and Fredrick, 2006; Rowe, 1986). Although there are exceptions, the majority of children's attention will be lost if the wait time is too long.

A Classroom Example of Wait Time

Ryan is sitting alone at the dramatic play center. This week's dramatic play center is based on the theme "The Great Outdoors." It is filled with wonderful props: a canteen, grill, child-sized tent, plastic ants, lawn furniture, and outdoor stuffed animals.

Mrs. Card holds up a colorful caterpillar and says, "Look Ryan! What do I have?" She follows her question with a five-second pause, along with an expectant look.

Ryan engages in joint attention by looking at the item and then at Mrs. Card. Seeing that she has Ryan's attention, Mrs. Card then points to the stuffed animal and states, "This is a colorful caterpillar; it has many legs. Can you count how many legs the colorful caterpillar has?"

Although Ryan does not verbally answer within five seconds, he does approach the caterpillar. Mrs. Card guides Ryan's hand and begins to count the caterpillar's legs out loud.

Adult/Peer Imitation

When preschool students imitate each other, it is more than just wanting to be like others; it is a way for them to practice and master new skills. Imitation also allows them to communicate with peers and adults, gaining important early social skills (Garfinkle and Schwartz, 2002) . For typically developing children, imitating others is something that comes naturally, but for children with autism it is another skill that has to be taught. Joint attention and peer imitation are connected; as a result, it is ideal for teachers to incorporate the two skills throughout the classroom setting (Ingersoll, 2008).

Here are a few tips for adult/peer imitation:

- With a small group of students, lead a "Simon Says" instruction. The teacher leads the group by saying, "Do what I do. Tap your head." Then model the action for the children. Continue going around the small group and have each child pick an action for the group to follow, starting with the same prompt, "Do what I do, _____" (Garfinkle and Schwartz, 2002).
- Be sure to give positive praise whenever the children imitate the action. Praise is important (Beauchat, Blamey, and Walpole, 2009)!
- If the child is not copying the action, use a full or partial physical prompt while verbally repeating the name of the desired action. Again, remember to praise when the child imitates peers (Garfinkle and Schwartz, 2002; Greenspan and Wieder, 2006).

- Encourage the child to imitate peers throughout the day. "Ryan. Look at what Suzy is doing. She is stacking blocks. Let's go stack blocks like Suzy" (Greenspan and Wieder, 2006).

A Classroom Example of Peer Imitation

Ryan is standing by Jeff and Evan at the sand tub center. He is watching the two children fill up plastic cups with sand and then dump them out to create sand hills for their toy trucks. Mrs. Card prompts Ryan to interact with Jeff and Evan by saying, "Ryan, try to do what the boys are doing."

Waiting five seconds for Ryan to respond, she then models filling up plastic cups and turning them upside-down. She then takes Ryan's hand and, using partial prompts, helps Ryan fill up the plastic cup with sand and then dump it out.

Throughout the interaction Mrs. Card says, "What a great sand hill you are making," giving positive praise to all the boys at the center. Soon, Ryan is making hills on his own! Mrs. Card observes Jeff telling Ryan, "Put a sand hill over there. Do what I am doing. That's right. Good job, Ryan!"

ADDITIONAL CLASSROOM STRATEGIES TO INCREASE COMMUNICATION AND SOCIAL SKILLS

Teachers that have children with ASD in their classrooms must provide extra support in order for their students to become more socially active. Teachers can use the following strategies to increase social and communication exchanges throughout the school day (Greenspan and Wieder, 2006; Leach and LaRocque, 2011).

Playful Block

In the playful block strategy, also known as playful obstruction, the teacher purposefully and playfully gets in the way of an object the child wants (Leach and LaRocque, 2011).

A Classroom Example of Playful Block

Ryan wants the book The Very Hungry Caterpillar, *which is located on the shelf behind where Mrs. Card is standing. Although Mrs. Card knows what Ryan wants, she continues to stand in front of the shelf to purposefully engage Ryan in social interaction. Ryan points to the shelf and bounces up and down. Mrs. Card asks, "What do you want?" Ryan responds by saying "book," and Mrs. Card happily moves out of the way so Ryan can pick up the book.*

Playful Arrangement

Playful arrangement, also known as playful construction, allows a teacher to turn the experience of a child playing alone into an opportunity for social engagement (Leach and LaRocque, 2011).

A Classroom Example of Playful Arrangement

Ryan is at the letter center picking up magnetic letters and placing them on the easel. Mrs. Card sees this as a great learning opportunity and heads over to Ryan. She says, "Ryan begins with the letter R. Can you find the letter R?"

Ryan searches through the plastic bin until he finds the letter R. He picks it up and places it on the easel. Mrs. Card exclaims, "Wonderful job, Ryan! You found the letter R."

Playful Negotiation

Playful negotiation goes hand-in-hand with playful block and arrangement. This strategy enables the teacher to extend or stretch out an interaction. This can be done through a meaningful play scenario (Leach and LaRocque, 2011).

A Classroom Example of Playful Negotiation

It is snack time in Mrs. Card's preschool classroom, and Ryan points for a juice box. Before handing him the juice box Mrs. Card asks, "What type of juice are you having today?" "Apple," says Ryan. "Yes, Ryan, you are having apple juice. What color is the apple?" Mrs. Card replies as she is tapping on the apple picture on the juice box.

Ryan looks up at the juice box and replies, "It's red." Smiling and nodding her head yes, Mrs. Card places the juice box in front of Ryan and continues to pass out snacks to the rest of the class.

CONCLUSION

Remember, any interactions with ASD children should be accompanied with exaggerated facial expressions, voice inflections, physical cues, and, above all, fun! When the evidenced-based joint attention strategies highlighted in this chapter are used in the classroom, *all* students benefit. They will be included in numerous meaningful emergent literacy interactions while increasing their joint attention and social skills. Like Mrs. Card, teachers will see an increase in the children's social and communication skills throughout the classroom.

An increase in joint attention skills leads to greater literacy gains by all children, no matter their ability level. Subsequently, the classroom environment becomes an inclusive one in which all students become part of the classroom community.

REFERENCES

American Psychiatric Association. (2014). *Diagnostic and statistical manual of mental disorders*. Fifth edition. Washington, DC: American Psychiatric Association.

Beauchat, K., Blamey, K., and Walpole, S. (2009). Building preschool children's language and literacy one storybook at a time. *Reading Teacher*, 63, 26–39.

Bruner, J. (1978). From communication to language: A psychological perspective. In I. Markova (Ed.), *The social context of language* (225–287). New York: Wiley.

Centers for Disease Control and Prevention. (2014). CDC estimates that 1 in 68 children has been identified with autism spectrum disorder (News Release). Retrieved from: https://www.cdc.gov/media/releases/2014/p0327-autism-spectrum-disorder.html.

Fielding-Barnsley, R., and Purdie, N. (2003). Early intervention in the home for children at risk of reading failure. *Support for Learning*, 18, 77–82. doi:10.1111/1467-9604.00284.

Garfinkle, A. N., and Schwartz, I. S. (2002). Peer imitation: Increasing social interactions in children with autism and other developmental disabilities in inclusive preschool classrooms. *Topics in Early Childhood Special Education*, 22, 26–38.

Greenspan, S. I., and Wieder, S. (2006). *Engaging autism: Helping children relate, communicate and think with the DIR floortime approach*. Cambridge, MA: Da Capo Press.

Hughes, T. A., and Fredrick, L. D. (2006). Teaching with students with learning disabilities using class wide peer tutoring and constant time delay. *Journal of Behavioral Education*, 15, 1–23, dio: 10.1007/s10864-005-9003-5.

Ingersoll, B. (2008). The social role of imitation in autism: Implications for the treatment of imitation deficits. *Infants and Young Children*, 21, 107–19.

Isaken, J., and Holth, P. (2009). An operant approach to teaching joint attention skills to children with autism. *Behavioral Interventions*, 24, 215–36. doi:10.1002/bin.292.

Johnston, S. S., McDonnell, A. P., and Hawken, L. S. (2008). Enhancing outcomes in early literacy for young children with disabilities: Strategies for success. *Intervention in School and Clinic*, 43, 210–17.

Jones, E. A., and Carr, E. C. (2004). Joint attention in children with autism: Theory and intervention. *Focus on Autism and Other Developmental Disabilities*, 19, 13–26.

Jones, E. A., and Feeley, K. M. (2007). Parent implemented joint attention intervention for preschoolers with autism. *American Journal of Speech-Language*, 3, 253–68.

Justice, L. M., and Ezell, H. K. (2002). Use of storybook reading to increase print awareness in at risk children. *American Journal of Speech-Language Pathology*, 11, 17–29. doi:10.1044/1058-0360 (2002/003).

Justice, L. M., and Kaderavek, J. (2002). Using shared storybook reading to promote emergent literacy. *Teaching Exceptional Children*, 34, 8–13.

Justice, L. M., and Pullen, P. C. (2003). Promising interventions for promoting emergent literacy skills: Three evidence-based approaches. *Topics in Early Childhood Special Education*, 23(3), 99–113.

Lane, H. B., and Wright, T. L. (2007). Maximizing the effectiveness of reading aloud. *International Reading Association*, 60, 668–75. doi:10.1598/RT.60.7.7.

Lanter, E., and Watson, L. R. (2008). Promoting literacy in students with ASD: The basic for the SLP. *Language, Speech, and Hearing Services in Schools*, 39, 33–43.

Leach, D., and LaRocque, M. (2011). Increasing social reciprocity in young children with autism. *Intervention in School and Clinic*, 4, 150–56.

Loveland, K., and Landry, S. (1986). Joint attention and language in autism and developmental language delay. *Journal of Autism and Developmental Disorder*, 16, 335–49.

Mirenda, P., and Iacono, T. (1988). Strategies for promoting augmentative and alternative communication in natural contexts with students with autism. *Focus on Autistic Behavior*, 3, 1–16.

Mundy, P. (1995). Joint attention and social-emotional approach behavior in children with autism. *Development and Psychopathology*, 7, 63–82.

Mundy, P., Sigman, M., and Kasari, C. (1990). A longitudinal study of joint attention and language development in autistic children. *Journal of Autism and Developmental Disorders*, 20, 115–28.

Murray, D. S., Creaghead, N. A., Manning-Courtney, P., Shear, P. K., Bean, J., and Prendeville, J. (2008). The relationship between joint attention and language in children with autism spectrum disorders. *Focus on Autism and Other Developmental Disabilities*, 23, 5–15. doi:10.1177/1088357607311443.

Pierce, D., Munier, V., and Myers, C. T. (2009). Informing early intervention through an occupational science description of infant–toddler interactions with home space. *American Journal of Occupational Therapy*, 63, 273–87.

Roberts, J., Jurgens, J., and Burchinal, M. (2005). The role of home literacy practices in preschool children's language and emergent literacy skills. *Journal of Speech, Language, and Hearing Research*, 48, 345–59.

Rocha, M. L., Schreibman, L., and Stahmer, A. C. (2007). Effectiveness of training parents to teach joint attention in children with autism. *Journal of Early Intervention*, 2, 154–72.

Rowe, M. B. (1986). Wait time: Slowing down may be a way of speeding up! *Journal of Teacher Education*, 37, 43–50.

Shedd, M. K., and Duke, N. K. (2008). The power of planning: Developing effective readalouds. *Beyond the Journal: Young Children on the Web*. Retrieved from http://www.naeyc.org/files/yc/file/200811/BTJReadingAloud.pdf.

Thurm, A., Lord, C., Lee, L., and Newschaffer, C. (2007). Predictors of language acquisition in preschool children with autism spectrum disorder. *Journal of Autism Developmental Disorders*, 37, 1721–35. doi:10.1007/s10803-006-0300-1.

Vismara, L. A., and Lyons, G. L. (2007). Using preservative interests to elicit joint attention behaviors in young children with autism: Theoretical and clinical implication for understanding motivation. *Journal of Positive Behavior Interventions*, 9, 214.

Whitehurst, G. J., Arnold, D. S., Epstein, J. N., Angell, A. L., Smith, M., and Fischel, J. E. (1994). A picture book reading intervention in day care and home for children from low-income families. *Developmental Psychology*, 30, 679–89.

Chapter Two

Mathematics Problem-Solving in Context

Improving Comprehension for Students with Mathematics Difficulty

Melissa Driver

Introduction Classroom Example: Mrs. Mack

Ms. Mack is a third-grade teacher in a diverse, inclusive classroom. She has several students with learning disabilities and several English Language Learners in her classroom. Ms. Mack's students demonstrate a range of mathematical understanding and often struggle to connect problem-solving procedures with their associated concepts. Recently, Ms. Mack taught an introductory lesson on division, a new concept for her third-grade students.

The lesson was a complete disaster—students left that day more confused than they began. By looking at their daily exit tickets, Ms. Mack can tell that some students have a basic understanding of the concept of division but can't calculate correctly, some students can perform the calculations correctly but have no understanding of the concept, and some students are missing both the concept and the procedure for solving division problems.

A common misconception is that mathematics instruction contains less literacy and language demand because it is a universal content. This could not be further from the truth. Consider Ms. Mack's division lesson. When introducing division, she might use several possible symbols to represent this new concept, such as the long division symbol, divisor symbol, fraction bar, and so forth.

In terms of her language, she might say several different words to describe the operation. For instance, she might tell students, "Put the larger number under the house and the smaller number outside the house," or she might ask, "How many times does the small number go into the big number?" The words she chooses and the words she omits have an impact on how her students learn the meaning of and process for division. In this example, and many others in mathematics, there are multiple steps to keep track of while problem solving. It can be challenging for students to comprehend the purpose and process of each step.

Students who experience persistent challenges with mathematics are often referred to by scholars as having mathematics difficulty. While only 3 percent to 6.5 percent of school-age students are formally diagnosed with a mathematics disability (Shalev, 2004), a much greater and often unknown percentage of students experience mathematics difficulty. Elementary students with mathematics difficulty may have problems with counting (Geary, Hamson, and Hoard, 2000), comparing numbers (De Smedt and Gilmore, 2011), working with number combinations (Jordan and Montani, 1997), basic computation (Chong and Siegel, 2008), and solving word problems (Reikerås, 2009).

Students with mathematics difficulty may also experience reading difficulty. Research indicates that both students with reading and mathematics difficulties and those with only mathematics difficulty struggle with higher-order problem solving (Hanich et al., 2011). Evidence-based instruction for students with mathematics difficulty includes explicit instruction (e.g., Flores and Kaylor, 2007; Fuchs et al., 2008; Jitendra et al., 2009) and instruction that connects mathematical concepts and procedures (Miller and Hudson, 2007).

The National Council of Teachers of Mathematics (NCTM) advocates for students to value mathematics, to become confident in their ability to do mathematics, to become mathematical problem solvers, to learn to communicate mathematically, and to learn to reason mathematically (Foegen and Deno, 2001). In terms of literacy, students are expected to read, analyze, and write mathematical text, such as numbers, symbols, and graphs (Siebert and Draper, 2008).

With the introduction of the Common Core State Standards for Mathematics (CCSSM), instruction now focuses more than ever on improving students' ability to reason, analyze, and interpret mathematical content across all grade levels (National Governors Association Center for Best Practices, 2010). Many teachers, however, are hesitant to integrate literacy practices specific to mathematics, possibly because they receive little instruction on how to do so in their preparation programs (Colwell and Enderson, 2016).

While the NCTM goals are important for all students, they are especially critical for culturally and linguistically diverse students, who consistently perform lower on standardized mathematics measures than their Caucasian, native-English-speaking peers (National Center for Education Statistics,

2013). In terms of postsecondary outcomes, African American and Latino students are underrepresented in science, technology, engineering, and mathematics college majors (Engberg and Wolniak, 2013).

Pursuing effective and equitable instructional approaches for culturally and linguistically diverse students and students with mathematics difficulty can promote achievement in elementary mathematics. Early success in mathematics is a strong predictor of later achievement in school (Morgan, Farkas, and Wu, 2011) and can lead to increased college and career opportunities (Murnane et al., 2001). In contrast, students with lower mathematics performance in school have fewer career opportunities as adults and make a lower income than adults with higher mathematics performance (Parsons and Bynner, 2005).

INCREASING COMPREHENSION THROUGH EVIDENCE-BASED MATHEMATICS INSTRUCTION

Research on the relationship between reading and mathematics indicates that reading comprehension may play a more important role in predicting mathematics performance than other aspects of literacy, such as phonological awareness, oral reading fluency, and so forth (Rutherford-Becker and Vanderwoord, 2009).

In this chapter, four instructional approaches to increase students' comprehension of and performance in mathematics are presented: explicitly teaching mathematics vocabulary, using schema instruction to teach metacognition and improve word-problem solving, encouraging oral and written communication, and connecting mathematics content to students' lives and critical issues. Each approach has the potential to increase both students' literacy and mathematics proficiency by increasing an understanding of the context in which students are solving problems.

EXPLICITLY TEACH MATHEMATICS VOCABULARY

Vocabulary acquisition is often associated with improved reading comprehension (Joshi, 2005). Increasing vocabulary for students with disabilities (Carlisle, Kenney, and Vereb, 2013; Ebbers and Denton, 2008) and English Language Learners (Lesaux et al., 2010) can improve overall comprehension of text.

Vocabulary also plays an important role in learning mathematics. Understanding mathematics vocabulary is connected to conceptual understanding (Capraro and Joffrion, 2006). Vocabulary instruction can be both direct (that is, instruction on unknown words) and indirect (that is, students develop understanding of terminology over time).

Mathematics vocabulary is often learned indirectly (Capraro and Joffrion, 2006). Evidence suggests, however, that students with learning difficulties benefit from explicit vocabulary instruction that incorporates keyword or mnemonic approaches, cognitive strategy instruction, and graphic organizers (Bryant et al., 2003; Jitendra et al., 2004). Content vocabulary instruction is most beneficial when delivered frequently, on a limited number of words, and in small groups (Bryant et al., 2003).

Explicit instruction is an effective approach for teaching students with learning disabilities across contents and grade levels (Flores and Kaylor, 2007; Rupley, Blair, and Nichols, 2009; Spencer, Goldstein, and Kaminski, 2012; Taylor et al., 2009). Explicit instruction for students with disabilities includes defining a task or objective, purposeful modeling by the teacher, frequent opportunities for student practice and application, and constant feedback throughout the lesson cycle (Archer and Hughes, 2011).

Strategies to explicitly introduce mathematics vocabulary and concepts to students include the following:

- Visuals and manipulatives
- Graphic organizers
- Examples and nonexamples
- Keywords and mnemonics
- Frequent and repeated exposure and practice

In mathematics instruction, teachers should explicitly introduce unfamiliar vocabulary, engage students in discussion about confusing terms, and encourage students to use mathematics vocabulary in their questions and conversations (Dunston and Tyminski, 2013).

There are four categories of mathematics terminology for teachers to consider in their instruction: (a) technical words that have one meaning, such as "circumference," (b) subtechnical words that have multiple meanings, such as "area," (c) general words common in everyday language that have a mathematical meaning, such as "reduce," and (d) symbolic words in which amounts are represented by abstract numerals or symbols, such as "plus" represented by "+" (Monroe and Panchyshyn, 1995).

Teachers should consider their students' prior experiences and understanding across each of these categories as they plan for vocabulary instruction, keeping in mind that what might be considered a "general" word for some students might be less familiar to students just learning English. In addition to the instructional strategies listed above, the following approaches can also support English Language Learners in learning mathematics vocabulary (Carlo et al., 2004; Garrison and Mora, 1999):

- Explicitly instructing students on morphology and cognates

- Using sentence starters and stems
- Acting out scenarios and problems
- Providing words in context
- Generating peer discussion

Symbols (such as +, -, and =) are often overlooked in mathematics vocabulary instruction, perhaps because teachers assume symbols are universal and devoid of language. However, research shows that students perform significantly worse on problems presented in abstract, symbolic form (such as 4 + __ = 8) than when the same problem is represented through manipulatives or pictures (Driver and Powell, 2015; Sherman and Bisanz, 2009).

This indicates that the presence of symbols and numerals in mathematics problems may confuse students, which can lead to misconceptions and difficulty solving more complex problems. For example, students often misinterpret the equal sign as an operational symbol—that is, find the answer; do something—instead of a relational symbol—that is, the two sides of this equation are the same (McNeil and Alibali, 2005). Such misinterpretation can lead to difficulty solving algebraic equations and word problems (Powell and Fuchs, 2010).

Teachers can foster correct symbolic understanding in several ways. First, mathematics instruction that connects abstract concepts to the values and processes they represent can help students visualize and correctly solve problems. One approach for doing so is the Concrete-Representation-Abstract (CRA) sequence, in which students first learn to represent and solve problems using tangible manipulatives (the concrete stage), then move to using pictures on paper (the representational stage) before finally solving equations with numerals and symbols (the abstract stage) (Miller and Hudson, 2007).

As students learn to connect concepts with procedures, teachers must be mindful of the language and vocabulary they use in instruction. Teachers should explicitly teach the meaning of symbols and not assume students will infer correct interpretations on their own. Additionally, exposure to and practice solving equations in nonstandard form (that is, equations in which the unknown is in varied positions) can help students develop appropriate symbolic understanding.

Students are typically presented with problems in standard form (for instance, 3 + 4 = __), and this repeated exposure may contribute to their misinterpretation of symbols. However, when nonstandard equations (for example, __ = 9 − 4; 2 + 3 = __ + 1; 5 = __) are included in instruction, students develop more accurate and appropriate understandings of the meaning behind mathematics symbols (McNeil et al., 2011; Powell, Driver, and Julian, 2015).

TEACH METACOGNITION: USING SCHEMAS TO RECOGNIZE
AND SOLVE WORD PROBLEMS

In addition to understanding the meaning of terminology and symbols used in mathematics instruction, students must be able to recognize when and how to apply appropriate procedures to solve problems. To do so, students must comprehend the context of those problems. This can be particularly challenging when solving word problems—that is, a mathematics calculation presented using words and sentences.

Word problems can be particularly challenging because students must use text to identify missing information, make a plan to solve the problem, and perform one or more calculations to get the solution (Powell, 2011). The language, unfamiliar contexts, and multistep processes inherent in word problems can pose a particular challenge for students with mathematics difficulty (Bryant, Bryant, and Hammill, 2000; Reikerås, 2009) and English Language Learners (Martiniello, 2008).

To effectively solve word problems students must comprehend the action occurring in the context of the problem and use appropriate strategies to solve for an unknown. Instructional approaches that teach students to rely on keywords, such as "more than" or "in all," often cause students to begin calculations without understanding the context. A promising, systematic approach for teaching students to solve word problems is schema instruction.

In the research, schema instruction is also called cognitively guided instruction (Ambrose and Molina, 2010), schema-based instruction (Jitendra et al., 2013), and schema-broadening instruction (Fuchs et al., 2008). This approach combines explicit strategy instruction and metacognition—that is, a person's awareness of strategies, organizing information, planning solution attempts, executing plans, and checking results (Goldberg and Bush, 2003)—to improve word-problem solving. The heart of schema instruction is teaching students to recognize common word-problem scenarios and to apply appropriate strategies to solve them.

In schema instruction, students are taught to identify problem types (such as Group, Change, Compare; Jitendra and Star, 2011), set up an equation that accurately reflects the problem type, and then solve for the unknown using appropriate strategies. Schema instruction can be used with both additive problems (addition and subtraction) and multiplicative problems (multiplication and division). For example, students can be taught to recognize three types of additive problems: Group, Change, and Compare.

A Group problem asks students to total two or more amounts; it is also called a Total, or Combine, problem. For example: Isabel has two apples and four bananas. How many pieces of fruit does she have? In a Change problem, students are given an initial amount, a change occurs, and students are asked to find the resulting amount.

Change problems can increase. For instance: Isabel has six apples. Her sister gave her three more apples. How many apples does Isabel have now? Or, alternatively, they can decrease. For example: Isabel has seven apples. She gave her sister two apples. How many apples does Isabel have now? A Compare, or Difference, problem prompts students to use the relationship between two quantities to find the unknown. For example: Isabel has four apples. Her sister has five more apples than Isabel. How many apples does Isabel's sister have?

Once students are taught to identify a problem type, they are instructed on specific strategies—that is, diagram, equation, or plan—to solve each type (Powell, 2011). Students are presented problems in varying formats and provided strategy instruction to solve each variation. For example, in a Change problem students can solve three variations: (a) the initial amount is unknown, (b) the change amount is unknown, or (c) the end amount is unknown.

Schema instruction is a well-validated approach for improving comprehension of and ability to correctly solve word problems for students with mathematics difficulty (Fuchs et al., 2008, 2009; Jitendra et al., 2009; Powell, 2011; Powell and Fuchs, 2010), and preliminary research shows promise for English Language Learners (Driver and Powell, 2016).

ENCOURAGE ORAL AND WRITTEN COMMUNICATION

As students learn mathematics vocabulary and metacognitive strategies to increase their comprehension, teachers should also strategically encourage oral and written communication to solidify student understandings. Communication is described as an essential part of mathematics and listed as one of the five NCTM process standards for effective communication (National Council of Teachers of Mathematics, 2000).

Similarly, the CCSSM require students to construct viable arguments, critique the mathematics reasoning of others, explain how to solve problems, use clear vocabulary, and communicate accurately to others (National Governors Association Center for Best Practices, 2010). Communication in elementary classrooms includes both oral and written communication.

Encouraging peer discussion and discourse around mathematical ideas can help students develop and solidify conceptual understandings and approaches to problem solving (Cross, 2009). Characteristics of effective mathematical discussions include students asking questions, contributing to the conversation, evaluating peer contributions, having their ideas evaluated, and receiving immediate feedback (Inagaki, Hatano, and Morita, 1998).

The teacher's role is to initiate and facilitate students in collaborative discussion and debate. Providing opportunities for discussion and discourse is particularly important for diverse learners, including English Language Learners, as they develop mathematical understanding in a new language (Moschkovish, 2008, 2013; Thompson, 2010).

Writing helps students develop, connect, and consolidate their thoughts and ideas and holds promise for helping students construct mathematical understandings. Integrating writing in mathematics may simultaneously increase both writing skill and mathematics understanding (Thompson, 2010). Having students write out their mathematical thinking can help them organize and connect ideas and can help teachers understand the cause of student errors (Cross, 2009; Thompson, 2010). Teachers can support students' writing in formal and informal ways:

- Mathematics journal or diary writing
- Exit slips or tickets
- Class books
- Think-write-shares
- Explaining your answer
- Evaluating other students' work
- Comparing and analyzing scenarios

Note that there is little empirical evidence regarding the best way to support student writing about mathematics. Further research is needed in this area (Powell and Hebert, 2016). Existing evidence suggests that mathematics computation and writing skills do not necessarily translate to success on mathematics writing prompts and that students may need to practice applying different combinations of writing and computation skills to specific mathematics-writing tasks (Powell and Hebert, 2016).

General writing strategies that help students plan, compose, and revise their writing, such as Self-Regulated Strategy Development, mnemonics, and graphic organizers (Mason, Harris, and Graham, 2011), and explicit instruction in mathematics computation may both be needed to improve students' ability to write about their mathematical literacy.

CONNECT MATHEMATICS CONTENT TO STUDENTS' LIVES AND CRITICAL ISSUES

In addition to the instructional approaches listed above, teachers should provide students with opportunities to solve problems in authentic and meaningful contexts. Culturally responsive mathematics instruction refers to pedagogical knowledge, teacher beliefs, and instructional practices that promote mathematical thinking, value student funds of knowledge and identity, and incorporate issues of power and social justice in mathematics education (Aguirre and del Rosario Zavala, 2013).

Connections between mathematics content and student lives should be meaningful and move beyond superficial acknowledgments of cultural holidays, celebrations, and the like (Banks, 2008). For example, presenting mathematical tasks that reflect scenarios and significant contexts for students is more effective than simply including student names or community locations in word problems.

Teachers can facilitate meaningful connections with both school-based and home- or community-based contexts. A simple place to start is with meaningful scenarios that students might encounter in their school:

- Calculating the length of time spent on independent reading and using this baseline to set weekly goals and graph progress.
- Conducting a survey of school lunch options at schools in neighboring districts and comparing the nutritional quality between zip codes.
- Measuring the distance of a classroom's fire escape route to determine if it is the fastest and safest and, if not, proposing an alternate route to the principal.

Each of these examples incorporates mathematics skills and concepts into relevant contexts to increase student comprehension of the task and engage them in ways that validate their voice and contribution to the greater school community. Building from school-based tasks, teachers should also seek to incorporate contexts that are meaningful to individual students and their communities. Funds of knowledge and identity refer to experiences and understandings that students bring into the classroom from their home community, such as measuring ingredients while cooking and the economic practices of a local business (Esteban-Guitart and Moll, 2014; Moll et al., 1992).

Student funds of knowledge and identity can be incorporated in mathematics instruction. However, in order to do so authentically, teachers must build meaningful relationships with students and their parents or guardians. This is particularly important for culturally and linguistically diverse students, whose lived experiences may be less represented in traditional school curriculum and textbooks.

Culturally responsive mathematics instruction should also move beyond students' individual experiences to analyze larger social issues that may affect students' lives. Turner and Strawhun (2007) show that in order to address complex issues of justice and equality, the contexts teachers present should generate problems that students find worth solving (such as using a mathematics measurement unit to analyze school overcrowding).

On a large scale, mathematics education can be used to analyze relationships of power and privilege through social and economic structures. Connecting mathematics content with students' lives can improve their understanding of the reading, writing, and oral language demands associated with the assigned task. Taking a culturally responsive approach to mathematics can deepen students' comprehension of mathematical concepts and procedures while reinforcing the importance of analysis and problem solving for creating change as individuals and as members of a larger community.

CONCLUSION

After analyzing her students' exit tickets, researching evidence-based practices, and discussing ideas with colleagues, Ms. Mack is excited to reintroduce division. First, she makes a list of the possible vocabulary terms and symbols students may encounter while solving division problems. From this list she considers which words and symbols she will explicitly teach and which she will reinforce through indirect conversations. She plans when she will introduce each vocabulary term and how students will practice throughout the unit.

Next, Ms. Mack identifies common problem types (that is, schemas) for division in the third-grade curriculum. She considers which schema makes sense to introduce first, researches aligned strategies for solving each problem type, and maps out a plan to teach each problem type throughout the unit. She double checks this with her vocabulary plan and adjusts as needed to ensure students have the necessary understandings throughout the unit.

Ms. Mack then considers how she will incorporate oral and written communication throughout each lesson of the division unit. She decides to have students keep a journal for this unit and notes prompts that might be good to use as think-write-shares. To encourage rich discussion, she brainstorms possible school-based scenarios around which she can design mathematics tasks to engage students in the purpose and relevance of division.

When thinking of possible home- and community-based scenarios, Ms. Mack realizes that she does not know her students quite as well as she assumed she did. She commits to building stronger relationships with her students and their families and is excited to begin doing so through this division unit.

In sum, teachers can improve students' comprehension of and proficiency in mathematics by increasing student understanding of the context in which they are solving problems. The instructional approaches presented in this chapter hold promise for all students, including students with persistent mathematics difficulty. Strengthening students' comprehension of mathematics concepts and procedures can improve both academic performance and engagement in this critical content area.

REFERENCES

Aguirre, J. M., and del Rosario Zavala, M. (2013). Making culturally responsive mathematics teaching explicit: A lesson analysis tool. *Pedagogies*, 8, 163–90. doi:10.1080/1554480X.2013.768518.

Ambrose, R., and Molina, M. (2010). First-grade Latino English Language Learners' performance on story problems in Spanish versus English. *Canadian Journal of Science, Mathematics, and Technology Education*, 10, 356–69. doi:10.1080/14926156.2010.524968.

Archer, A. L., and Hughes, C. A. (2011). *Explicit instruction: Effective and efficient teaching.* New York: Guilford.

Banks, J. A. (2008). Curriculum transformation. In J. A. Banks, *An introduction to multicultural education*, fourth edition. New York: Pearson.

Bryant, D., Bryant, B. R., and Hammill, D. D. (2000). Characteristic behaviors of students with LD who have teacher-identified math weaknesses. *Journal of Learning Disabilities*, 33, 168–77. doi:10.1177/002221940003300205.

Bryant, D. P., Goodwin, M., Bryant, B. R., and Higgins, K. (2003). Vocabulary instruction for students with learning disabilities: A review of the research. *Learning Disability Quarterly*, 26, 117–28. doi:10.2307/1593594.

Capraro, M., and Joffrion, H. (2006). Algebraic equations: Can middle-school students meaningfully translate from words to mathematical symbols? *Reading Psychology*, 27(2–3), 147–64.

Carlisle, J. F., Kenney, C. K., and Vereb, A. (2013). Vocabulary instruction for students at risk for reading disabilities: Promising approaches for learning from texts. In D. C. Chard, B. G. Cook, and M. G. Tankersley (Eds.), *Research-based strategies for improving outcomes in academics* (47–60). Upper Saddle River, NJ: Pearson.

Carlo, M. S., August, D., McLaughlin, B., Snow, C. E., Dressler, C., Lippman, D. N., and White, C. E. (2004). Closing the gap: Addressing the vocabulary needs of English-language learners in bilingual and mainstream classrooms. *Reading Research Quarterly*, 39(2), 188–215.

Chong, S. L., and Siegel, L. S. (2008). Stability of computational deficits in math learning disability from second through fifth grades. *Developmental Neuropsychology*, 33, 300–317. doi:10.1080/87565640801982387.

Colwell, J., and Enderson, M. C. (2016). "When I hear literacy": Using pre-service teachers' perceptions of mathematical literacy to inform program changes in teacher education. *Teaching and Teacher Education*, 53, 63–74.

Cross, D. I. (2009). Creating optimal mathematics learning environments: Combining argumentation and writing to enhance achievement. *International Journal of Science and Mathematics Education*, 7(5), 905–30.

De Smedt, B., and Gilmore, C. K. (2011). Defective number module or impaired access? Numerical magnitude processing in first graders with mathematical difficulties. *Journal of Experimental Child Psychology*, 108, 278–92. doi:10.1016/j.jecp.2010.09.003.

Driver, M. K., and Powell, S. R. (2015). Symbolic and nonsymbolic equivalence tasks: The influence of symbols on students with mathematics difficulty. *Learning Disabilities Research and Practice*, 30, 127–34.

Driver, M. K., and Powell, S. R. (May 2016). Culturally and linguistically responsive schema intervention: Improving word-problem solving for English Language Learners with mathematics difficulty. *Learning Disability Quarterly*. Published online ahead of print. doi:10.1177/0731948716646730.

Dunston, P., and Tyminski, A. (2013). What's the big deal about vocabulary? *Mathematics Teaching in the Middle School*, 19(1), 38–45.

Ebbers, S. M., and Denton, C. A. (2008). A root awakening: Vocabulary instruction for older students with reading difficulties. *Learning Disabilities Research and Practice*, 23, 90–102.

Engberg, M. E., and Wolniak, G. C. (2013). College student pathways to the STEM disciplines. *Teachers College Record*, 115(1). Retrieved from Loyola eCommons, School of Education: Faculty Publications and Other Works, http://ecommons.luc.edu/education_facpubs/10.

Esteban-Guitart, M., and Moll, L. C. (2014). Funds of identity: A new concept based on the funds of knowledge approach. *Culture and Psychology*, 20, 31–48. doi:10.1177/13540 67X13515934.

Flores, M. M., and Kaylor, M. (2007). The effects of a direct instruction program on the fraction performance of middle school students at-risk for failure in mathematics. *Journal of Instructional Psychology*, 34, 84–94.

Foegen, A., and Deno, S. L. (2001). Identifying growth indicators for low-achieving students in middle school mathematics. *Journal of Special Education*, 35, 4–16.

Fuchs, L. S., Powell, S. R., Seethaler, P. M., Cirino, P. T., Fletcher, J. M., Fuchs, D., Hamlett, C. L., and Zumeta, R. O. (2009). Remediating number combination and word problem deficits among students with mathematics difficulties: A randomized control trial. *Journal of Educational Psychology*, 101, 561–76. doi:10.1037/a0014701.

Fuchs, L. S., Seethaler, P. M., Powell, S. R., Fuchs, D., Hamlett, C. L., and Fletcher, J. M. (2008). Effects of preventative tutoring on the mathematical problem solving of third-grade students with math and reading difficulties. *Exceptional Children*, 74, 155–73.

Garrison, L., and Kerper Mora, J. (1999). Adapting mathematics instruction for English-language learners: The Language-concept connection. In L. Ortiz-Franco, N. G. Hernandez, and Y. De La Cruz (Eds.), *Changing the Faces of Mathematics: Perspectives on Latinos* (35–47). Reston, VA: NCTM.

Geary, D. C., Hamson, C. O., and Hoard, M. K. (2000). Numerical and arithmetical cognition: A longitudinal study of process and concepts deficits in children with a learning disability. *Journal of Experimental Child Psychology*, 77, 236–63. doi:10.1006/jecp.2000.2561.

Goldberg, P. D., and Bush, W. S. (2003). Using metacognitive skills to improve 3rd graders' math problem solving. *Focus on Learning Problems in Mathematics*, 25(4), 36.

Hanich, L. B., Jordan, N. C., Kaplan, D., and Dick, J. (2001). Performance across different areas of mathematical cognition in children with learning difficulties. *Journal of Educational Psychology*, 93(3), 615–26.

Inagaki, K., Hatano, G., and Morita, E. (1998). Construction of mathematical knowledge through whole-class discussion. *Learning and Instruction*, 8(6), 503–26.

Jitendra, A. K., Edwards, L. L., Sacks, G., and Jacobson, L. A. (2004). What research says about vocabulary instruction for students with learning disabilities. *Exceptional Children*, 70, 299–322. doi:10.1177/001440290407000303.

Jitendra, A. K., Rodriguez, M., Kanive, R., Huang, J., Church, C., Corroy, K. A., and Zaslofsky, A. (2013). Impact of small-group tutoring interventions on the mathematical problem solving and achievement of third-grade students with mathematics difficulties. *Learning Disability Quarterly*, 36, 21–35. doi:10.1177/0731948712457561.

Jitendra, A. K., and Star, J. R. (2011). Meeting the needs of students with learning disabilities in inclusive mathematics classrooms: The role of schema-based instruction on mathematical problem-solving. *Theory into Practice*, 50, 12–19. doi:10.1080/00405841.2011.534912.

Jitendra, A. K., Star, J. R., Starosta, K., Leh, J. M., Sood, S., Caskie, G., and Mack, T. R. (2009). Improving seventh grade students' learning of ratio and proportion: The role of schema-based instruction. *Contemporary Educational Psychology*, 34, 250–64.

Jordan, N. C., and Montani, T. O. (1997). Cognitive arithmetic and problem solving: A comparison of children with specific and general mathematics difficulties. *Journal of Learning Disabilities*, 30, 624–34. doi:10.1177/002221949703000606.

Joshi, R. (2005). Vocabulary: A critical component of comprehension. *Reading and Writing Quarterly*, 21(3), 209–19.

Lesaux, N. K., Kieffer, M. J., Faller, S. E., and Kelley, J. G. (2010). The effectiveness and ease of implementation of an academic vocabulary intervention for linguistically diverse students in urban middle schools. *Reading Research Quarterly*, 45, 196–228.

Martiniello, M. (2008). Language and the performance of English-Language Learners in math word problems. *Harvard Educational Review*, 78(2), 333–68.

Mason, L. H., Harris, K. R., and Graham, S. (2011). Self-regulated strategy development for students with writing difficulties. *Theory into Practice*, 50(1), 20–27.

McNeil, N. M., and Alibali, M. W. (2005). Why won't you change your mind? Knowledge of operational patterns hinders learning and performance on equations. *Child Development*, 76(4), 883–99.

McNeil, N. M., Fyfe, E. R., Petersen, L. A., Dunwiddie, A. E., and Brletic-Shipley, H. (2011). Benefits of practicing 4 = 2 + 2: Nontraditional problem formats facilitate children's understanding of mathematical equivalence. *Child Development*, 82, 1620–33.

Miller, S. P., and Hudson, P. J. (2007). Using evidence-based practices to build mathematics competence related to conceptual, procedural, and declarative knowledge. *Learning Disabilities Research and Practice*, 22, 47–57.

Moll, L. C., Amanti, C., Neff, D., and González, N. (1992). Funds of knowledge for teaching: Using a qualitative approach to connect homes and classrooms. *Theory into Practice*, 31, 132–41. doi:10.1080/00405849209543534.

Monroe, E. E., and Panchyshyn, R. (1995). Vocabulary considerations for teaching mathematics. *Childhood Education*, 72, 80–83. doi:10.1080/00094056.1996.10521849.

Morgan, P. L., Farkas, G., and Wu, Q. (2011). Kindergarten children's growth trajectories in reading and mathematics: Who falls increasingly behind? *Journal of Learning Disabilities*, 44, 472–88. doi:10.1177/0022219411414010.

Moschkovich, J. N. (2008). "I went by twos, he went by one": Multiple interpretations of inscriptions as resources for mathematical discussions. *Journal of the Learning Sciences*, 17, 551–87. doi:10.1080/10508400802395077.

Moschkovich, J. N. (2013). Principles and guidelines for equitable mathematics teaching practices and materials for English Language Learners. *Journal of Urban Mathematics Education*, 6, 45–57.

Murnane, R. J., Willett, J. B., Braatz, M. J., and Duhaldeborde, Y. (2001). Do different dimensions of male high school students' skills predict labor market success a decade later? Evidence from the NLSY. *Economics of Education Review*, 20, 311–20. doi:10.1016/s0272-7757(00)00056-x.

National Center for Education Statistics. (2013). *The nation's report card: A first look—2013 mathematics and reading* (NCES 2014–451). Washington, DC: Institute of Education Sciences, U.S. Department of Education.

National Council of Teachers of Mathematics (2000). *Principles and standards for school mathematics*. Reston, VA: NCTM.

National Governors Association Center for Best Practices, Council of Chief State School Officers (2010). *Common core state standards (Mathematics)*. Washington, DC: National Governors Association Center for Best Practices, Council of Chief State School Officers.

Parsons, S., and Bynner, J. (2005). *Does numeracy matter more?* Report for the National Research and Development Centre for Adult Literacy and Numeracy Institute of Education, University of London.

Powell, S. R. (2011). Solving word problems using schemas: A review of the literature. *Learning Disabilities Research and Practice*, 26, 94–108. doi:10.1111/j.1540-5826.2011.00329.x.

Powell, S. R., Driver, M. K., and Julian, T. E. (2015). The effect of tutoring with nonstandard equations on the mathematics performance of second-grade students with mathematics difficulty. *Journal of Learning Disabilities*, 48(5), 523–34.

Powell, S. R., and Fuchs, L. S. (2010). Contribution of equal-sign instruction beyond word-problem tutoring for third-grade students with mathematics difficulty. *Journal of Educational Psychology*, 102, 381–94.

Powell, S. R., and Hebert, M. A. (2016). Influence of writing ability and computation skill on mathematics writing. *Elementary School Journal*, 117(2), 310–35.

Reikerås, E. K. L. (2009). A comparison of performance in solving arithmetical word problems by children with different levels of achievement in mathematics and reading. *Investigations in Mathematics Learning*, 1, 49–72.

Rupley, W. H., Blair, T. R., and Nichols, W. D. (2009). Effective reading instruction for struggling readers: The role of direct/explicit teaching. *Reading and Writing Quarterly*, 25, 125–38. doi:10.1080/10573560802683523.

Rutherford-Becker, K. J., and Vanderwood, M. L. (2009). Evaluation of the relationship between literacy and mathematics skills as assessed by curriculum-based measures. *California School Psychologist*, 14(1), 23–34.

Shalev, R. S. (2004). Developmental dyscalculia. *Journal of Child Neurology*, 19, 765–71.

Sherman, J., and Bisanz, J. (2009). Equivalence in symbolic and non-symbolic contexts: Benefits of solving problems with manipulatives. *Journal of Educational Psychology*, 101, 88–100.

Siebert, D., and Jo Draper, R. (2008). Why content-area literacy messages do not speak to mathematics teachers: A critical content analysis. *Literacy Research and Instruction*, 47(4), 229–45.

Spencer, E. J., Goldstein, H., and Kaminski, R. (2012). Teaching vocabulary in storybooks: Embedding explicit vocabulary instruction for young children. *Young Exceptional Children*, 15, 18–32. doi:10.1177/1096250611435367.

Taylor, D. B., Mraz, M., Nichols, W. D., Rickelman, R. J., and Wood, K. D. (2009). Using explicit instruction to promote vocabulary learning for struggling readers. *Reading and Writing Quarterly*, 25, 205–20. doi:10.1080/10573560802683663.

Thompson, L. S. (2010). Writing to communication mathematically in the elementary school classroom. *Ohio Journal of School Mathematics*, 61, 36–44.

Turner, E. E., and Strawhun, B. T. F. (2007). Posing problems that matter: Investigating school overcrowding. *Teaching Children Mathematics*, 13, 457–63.

Chapter Three

Literacy and the Gifted

Joanna Simpson

Introduction Classroom Example: Jillian

Jillian was eighteen months old when she learned to read sheet music. Her father was a composer and often left sheets lying around, along with notes and scrap paper on which he had brainstormed new pieces. Her aunt realized she was reading the sheet music when Jillian began to bang out a tune on her toy xylophone. This was the first clue that Jillian was musically gifted. Later, when Jillian struggled to read anything outside of poetry or songs that were set to music, her family and teachers were perplexed. Jillian was in the gifted program and could complete accelerated coursework. How could a child who was labeled gifted struggle to comprehend basic grade-level text? It didn't make sense to them. Maybe she wasn't trying? Maybe she wasn't motivated? It couldn't have anything to do with her ability, could it? Gifted kids are supposed to succeed in everything, right?

There are many misconceptions when it comes to gifted learners. In the case of literacy, not all gifted learners are gifted readers. Children who have an exceptional ability to read and work with text are considered gifted readers (Mason and Au, 1990). Gifted readers read voraciously, perform well above their grade level, possess advanced vocabularies, and do well on tests (Vacca, Vacca, and Gove, 1991).

Gifted readers usually have advanced language abilities in comparison to other children of the same age. They use words easily, accurately, and creatively in new and innovative contexts and speak in semantically complex and syntactically complicated sentences (Bond and Bond, 1983). Their cognitive ability mirrors their language ability; therefore, the cognitive abilities of gifted readers vary from the norm. Those gifted in reading have a unique ability to perceive relationships, solve problems, demonstrate observational skills, and grasp abstract ideas quickly (Witty, 1981).

GIFTEDNESS

"Gifted" is an elusive label. Schools use various measures to determine giftedness. While the gifted population is quite diverse and cannot be reduced to a definitive list of characteristics, those labeled as gifted by schools tend to be intellectually or academically gifted (Reis and Renzulli, 2009, 2010; Sternberg and Zhang, 1995). It is unusual for schools to identify and label students who are gifted in an area other than academics, such as athletics or the arts, unless they are advanced academically as well.

In general, "gifted" is a label for people with significantly advanced cognition who reflect this advancement academically, artistically, or through interpersonal skills (Reis and Renzulli, 2009, 2010). Among the intellectually gifted, there are variations in skills and attributes; however, there are some attributes somewhat common among them: the ability to learn quickly, the capacity to comprehend abstract and complex concepts, and an advanced aptitude for problem-solving (Reis and Renzulli, 2009, 2010). Gifted children typically think divergently, process information in unique ways, learn basic skills quickly, comprehend abstract ideas, enjoy figuring out relationships, like complexity, show intense curiosity, use advanced vocabularies, and seek fairness (National Association of Gifted Children, 2008b). These characteristics are critical for schools to nurture.

Clark (1983) outlined intellectual needs that differentiated gifted children from others. These are the needs teachers must focus on when instructing gifted students:

- To be exposed to new and challenging information about the environment and the culture
- To be exposed to varied subjects and concerns
- To be allowed to pursue ideas as far as their interests take them
- To encounter and use increasingly difficult vocabulary and concepts
- To be exposed to ideas at rates appropriate to the individual's pace of learning
- To pursue inquiries beyond allotted time spans

GIFTED READERS

Many children who enter school knowing how to read are later identified as gifted. Approximately half of the children classified as gifted by intelligence tests could read in kindergarten, and nearly all of them could read at the beginning of first grade (Burns and Broman, 1983). Their literacy may develop naturally, without formal instruction, in home environments where reading is valued and language usage is encouraged (Durkin, 1966). Often, these children have been immersed in a print-rich environment and have "puzzled-out" for themselves how to read (Teale, 1982).

Gifted readers are often so advanced that they have little to gain from the reading materials and activities normally given to others of their age and grade. They require far less drill and practice than their peers (Witty, 1985). However, gifted readers have special needs just as other exceptional learners do. As discussed earlier in this chapter, it is critical for educators to be aware of and address those needs.

The greater the ability in reading, the greater the need for a special program commensurate with that ability (Hoskisson and Tompkins, 1987; Wallen, 1974). This does not necessarily have to be a software program or a program purchased specifically for advanced readers. It simply means these students need their teachers to differentiate for them. They need access to reading material that will challenge them without frustrating them.

Gifted readers will benefit from special programs and, unfortunately, may be penalized if not provided with special attention to help them achieve their full potential (Tuttle et al., 1988). These penalties come in the form of poor grades that can result when gifted readers are bored and intentionally underachieve or lose interest in reading altogether. In short, gifted readers need the same diagnostically based instruction that should be afforded to all learners (Bond and Bond, 1983; Carr, 1984; Rupley, 1984).

DIFFERENTIATION FOR GIFTED READERS

Reading teachers are concerned about providing quality differentiated instruction for the highly able readers in their classrooms. A logical means for providing such instruction is ability grouping, in which children with similar abilities are placed in the same group to work on a text or project. Gifted readers could be grouped together so they can feel safe in verbalizing and sharing their insights (Sakiey, 1980); such grouping has been found to increase their understanding and appreciation of literature.

Sometimes, teachers put gifted readers together with struggling readers so that the gifted readers can "teach" the struggling readers. This is an egregious mistake when dealing with gifted students, one that may lead to underachievement because the gifted students feel penalized for being advanced. Gifted students may become frustrated with the struggling readers and with the fact that they are expected to do the bulk of the work. Furthermore, the gifted readers are not exploring the text more deeply and are not furthering their own learning when they slow down to help the struggling readers.

Researchers (Bartelo and Cornette, 1982; Bigaj, 1968; Sakiey, 1980) have presented some general guidelines for working with gifted students:

- Instruction in basic word attitude skills should be kept to a minimum.
- Challenging materials should be made available, especially to young gifted readers.
- Instruction should facilitate critical and creative reading.
- Analogies should be studied, especially in classes for older gifted students.
- Instruction should be inductive rather than deductive.
- Assignments should be flexible.
- Unnecessary repetition in instructions should be eliminated.
- Students' divergent and diversified interests should be nurtured.
- Independent projects such as models, newscasts, games based on story themes, and simulation role-playing activities should be encouraged.

Shaughnessy (1994) recommended expanded literacy activities for the gifted as well, such as guest speakers in the classroom, creative writing, and connecting books with television or movies. These are easy ways to differentiate the curriculum when gifted students have been mainstreamed in a general education classroom. This happens often because funding for specialized gifted programs is scarce. In lieu of specialized programs or schools, gifted students are often accelerated or skipped a grade, or they are mainstreamed and a teacher is asked to differentiate for them.

Reading acceleration and individual enrichment are additional avenues for meeting the needs of gifted readers in the classroom (Karnes and Johnson, 1987). Reading acceleration places students on their instructional level in reading without regard to grade placement. If a kindergartner is reading at a third-grade level, the teacher would provide the kindergartner with a book recommended for third graders. Enrichment delves deeper into reading material at the student's grade level through extension activities or special projects on the material the student has mastered. If the kindergartener reading at a third-grade level has finished a story about the Three Billy Goats Gruff, for instance, an extension activity might be a play in which the student narrates or acts out the story. All reading levels of students can be involved, but the gifted reader would be challenged with the most lines, as an example.

Renzulli (1988) recommends that activities for the gifted emphasize higher-level thinking skills, controversial issues, and less-structured teaching. He also suggests heavy emphasis on higher levels of thinking, critical reading, vocabulary development, wide exposure to literature, productive thinking, imaginative thinking, visualization, exploration of values, and a language arts approach. Frezise (1978) advises rapid pacing and timing: "going deeper" into a topic, less rigidly structured learning environments, and provisions for critical thinking, reading, and writing.

Specific instructional programs for gifted readers vary from school to school and district to district. The most common programs specially designed for the gifted are described below.

- The triad enrichment model (Renzulli, 1977) provides gifted children with the opportunity for self-directed reading and independent study. The enrichment triad consists of three types of activities: (1) exploratory activities in which students investigate avenues of interest and then decide on a topic or problem to study in depth, (2) activities in which students are provided with the technical skills and thinking processes needed to investigate the research topic or problem, (3) investigative activities in which students explore their topic or solve their problem through individual or small-group work. Students then develop an end product that reflects their learning.
- Inquiry reading (Cassidy, 1981) also enables gifted readers to conduct research on topics of interest. In this four-week program for grades three and up, students select a topic, carry out research, and present their findings to others. The approach can be used by classroom teachers during the time usually reserved for basal reading instruction.
- Trevise (1984) recommends that teachers have gifted readers read and discuss literacy classics as part of the Junior Great Books Reading and Discussion Program. Junior Great Books is a highly developed, structured program encouraging careful reading of complex materials. Discussions of the readings are designed to be challenging and interesting and to focus on the universal themes present in the books.

Other recommended instructional models for gifted readers include Accelerated Individual Model of Enrichment (AIME) (Swaby, 1982), reading-strategy lessons (Goodman, Burke and Sherman, 1980), Direct Reading Teacher Activity (DRTA) (Bates, 1984), and vocabulary development through literature (Howell, 1987).

TECHNOLOGY AND CHALLENGES

Based on the citation dates in this chapter up to this point, the reader may note that many of these models for gifted readers are quite old. Figuring out how to teach gifted learners is not a new problem. Figuring out how to differentiate both for gifted learners who are advanced readers and for those who are not advanced readers is not a new problem either. However, since the research that has been conducted and cited in this chapter, there has been a major advance in teaching and learning that has helped to differentiate for gifted learners—technology.

Although technology offers more options to challenge gifted young minds, designing the instruction and assessing the final product present challenges too. Teachers often feel pressured to bring everyone to a level of minimum competency and may have little time to design challenging and engaging instruction for their gifted students (Law and Kaufhold, 2009; Loveless, Parkas, and Duffet, 2008).

Accessing and evaluating resources to use and designing appropriate curriculum are time-consuming, complex tasks that require an understanding of the nature and needs of gifted children. Gifted education is typically a specialty area that teachers would need to pursue as part of their higher education; as a result, few teachers understand the nature and needs of gifted children and can properly design curriculum for them.

Educators have been advocating for differentiated instruction, which entails giving students "equally challenging" work, not "equal" work. Tailoring instruction to individual strengths and needs is a worthwhile effort but can tax teachers with diverse classrooms and limited time and resources. With the emphasis on high-stakes testing and teacher accountability systems, the bulk of the teachers' time often goes to struggling students.

As the world becomes more global, the United States of America needs to tap into the great American ingenuity to stay competitive. The brightest and most talented have always led the way. When we do not differentiate for our students, we do so at our own peril. Yet, taking time away from struggling students cannot be the answer either. How, then, can we provide appropriately challenging instruction for gifted students? Finding a solution is critical.

Reading is one required area of instruction that affects all other disciplines. Teachers must address reading skills regardless of the wide range of reading abilities among students. One persistent problem facing teachers in regular elementary classrooms is how to differentiate instruction appropriately to meet the reading needs of gifted students with limited time, training, and resources. One strategy teachers may find helpful, and possibly more accessible, is a specialized online intervention that teachers can incorporate into the curriculum with very little time and effort.

The self-contained online intervention may include tracking and opportunities to provide individualized feedback to students. Student participants explore literature and language in a self-paced, nonlinear way, creating unique connections to text, self, and the world. They can also connect and collaborate with their like-minded peers in response to literature. The regular classroom teacher could employ an online instructional environment to both extend and enrich the regular language arts curriculum as a way of differentiating instruction for gifted students.

Gifted children in general learn more quickly, more deeply, and with more complexity than their same-age peers, and they also have greater problem-solving skills, task commitment, and ability (National Association of

Gifted Children, 2008a; Renzulli, 2005; Renzulli et al., 2002; Reis and Renzulli, 2009, 2010). Most definitions of giftedness include the students' need for instruction that differs from their same-age peers (Marland, 1972; Sternberg et al., 1996). An appropriately differentiated curriculum for gifted students requires modified instruction (content, process, delivery, measures, and product) aligned with the unique needs of individual gifted students. There are a number of obstacles that hinder general education teachers from implementing such adjustments within the regular classroom setting; technology may hold the key to overcoming them.

NOT *REALLY* TEACHING COMPREHENSION

In 1978, Dolores Durkin published results of an eye-opening study that indicated explicit instruction of reading comprehension was noticeably lacking in classrooms (Durkin, 1978). Durkin had read three assumptions in the National Institute of Education's request for proposals that caught her eye. One in particular was the assumption that general education instructors teach reading comprehension. Her personal impression from years of classroom observations was that this was not the case. Reading teachers are teaching reading comprehension, and only those students who struggle with reading are put in the specialized reading class with a reading teacher.

An observational study (1978) confirmed Durkin's fears. Similar studies such as that conducted by Pressley and Wharton-McDonald twenty years later found similar results (as cited in Duke and Pearson, 2008/2009). In the last few decades, however, much research has gone into understanding what good readers do and how to teach those strategies to all students. Unlike research regarding teaching decoding and reading readiness, research on reading comprehension has not been fraught with debate.

Despite the smooth road of research to provide classroom teachers with effective teaching strategies, accountability systems have had the unfortunate outcome of emphasizing lower-level instruction (Law and Kaufhold, 2009; Loveless, Parkas, and Duffet, 2008). Even questions on high-stakes tests portrayed as higher level are not as challenging as the test writers have purported, leading teachers to believe they are already teaching higher-order comprehension skills. If students are passing the tests that teachers are told evaluate students' ability to comprehend text, there is little reason for teachers to think that their students lack comprehension skills.

In 1956, Benjamin Bloom designed a hierarchical representation of thinking that moves from lower-level thinking to higher-level thinking. His taxonomy has been used extensively in designing curriculum and instructional activities. A chart of verbs organized by Bloom's levels to formulate a question or task is readily available to teachers. One will often find such charts taped to teachers' desks or used in poster format.

In an attempt to make the taxonomy user-friendly for teachers, however, the model has become oversimplified, leading teachers and their evaluators to the misperception that they are teaching higher-level reading comprehension by using verbs in the top three levels to generate questions and activities (Parks, 2009). With this simplistic approach, an assignment to compare and contrast two characters from a story is commonly categorized as an analysis activity. That was never the intention of Bloom's taxonomy. Rather, Bloom intended for analysis to include abstract inferences, distinguish cause and effect from sequence, and generate processes such as "recognizing unstated assumptions, distinguishing fact from hypothesis, and distinguishing a conclusion from statements that support it" (Parks, 2009, p. 264).

Based on this description of analysis, a typical compare/contrast question in which students list descriptors for similarities and differences does not fit in this category. VanTassel-Baska and Stambaugh's textbook, *Comprehensive Curriculum for Gifted Learners* (2006), provides several suggestions for adapting regular classroom activities to fit Bloom's description of analysis. It is a bit more in depth than choosing the correct verb.

The authors suggest critical discussion topics for regular instruction and a correlating challenge discussion topic for gifted readers. For example, a lower-level question might ask, "Have any of the characters changed over the course of your readings? Explain your answer." The higher-level question might ask, "Which of the generalizations about change most reflects your reading? Justify your answer with examples." The higher-level question requires understanding the criteria of the generalizations for the concept of change and providing support.

Similar errors arise with evaluation tasks. Parks states that some issues "in using the Bloom model [have] been lack of clarity about critical thinking processes, lack of explicitness in teaching them, and underdeveloped standards for evaluating how adequately one is thinking through a complex issue" (2009, p. 264). Educators often believe that asking students to evaluate a text requires higher-level thinking.

However, if students do not already know the criteria, methods of analysis, and elements and organizational principles commonly used by experts within the related field for evaluation, they are simply demonstrating comprehension of the passage. Comprehension is very different than analysis.

If teachers believe they are having students analyze the text when they are in fact reflecting comprehension of the text, are they differentiating for gifted readers? No. That becomes a problem on exams where it is perceived that higher-order thinking is assessed, but gifted students are still completing them quickly without struggle. We are not measuring what we think we are measuring.

Classroom teachers receive simplified charts of verbs without an in-depth understanding of higher-level thinking. Moreover, the tests for which teachers are held accountable claim to include higher-order thinking skills by asking what are in reality lower-level questions. Without proper materials to teach or assess these skills, it is no wonder that differentiation for higher-order thinking is nonexistent in many classrooms.

To press instruction into higher-level thinking, one could turn to literature in gifted education. However, the regular classroom teacher may never have seen these instructional models or may have ignored them, thinking that these strategies were useful only for gifted children. Dispelling the myths of higher-level comprehension takes time and effort. Providing teachers with ready-made, truly higher-order literacy instruction would provide a model for teachers ensuring that gifted students receive literacy instruction pushing them to their potential.

CONCLUSION

Gunning (1992) provides an excellent summary of the characteristics of a model program for gifted readers: "To grow intellectually, gifted students need challenging books. They need fiction with complex plots and carefully developed characters, and informational books that explore topics in depth. They should read books and periodicals that spark their imaginations, broaden their horizons, and cause them to wonder and question." Equity demands that the exceptionality of gifted readers be recognized and that appropriate programs designed to meet their unique needs be made available. All students, including those gifted in reading, deserve an educational program designed to help each individual achieve his or her full potential.

REFERENCES

Adomat, D. S. (2012). Becoming characters: Deepening young children's literary understanding through drama. *Journal of Children's Literature*, 38(1), 44–51.

Alessi, S. M., and Trollip, S. R. (2001). *Multimedia for learning: Methods and development.* Third edition. Needham Heights, MA: Allyn and Bacon.

Allen, M. W. (2006). *Creating successful e-learning: A rapid system for getting it right first time, every time.* San Francisco: Pfeiffer.

American Educational Research Association, American Psychological Association, and National Council on Measurement in Education. (1999). *Standards for educational and psychological testing.* Washington, DC.

American Educational Research Association and American Statistical Association. (2005). *Guidelines for assessment and instruction in statistics education: College report.* Alexandria, VA.

Anderson, T., and Shattuck, J. (2012). Design-based research: A decade of progress in education research? *Educational Researcher*, 41(1), 16–25.

Archambault, F. X., Jr., et al. (1993). *Regular classroom practices with gifted students: Results of a national survey of classroom teachers.* Research Monograph 93101. Storrs: National Research Center on the Gifted and Talented, University of Connecticut.

Ball, A. F. (2012). To know is not enough: Knowledge, power, and the Zone of Generativity. *Educational Researcher*, 41(8), 283–93.

Bartelo, D., and Cornette, J. (1982). *A literature program for the gifted.* ERIC Document Reproduction Service, ED 233333.

Bates, G. (1984). Developing reading strategies for the gifted: A research based approach. *Journal of Reading*, 27, 590–93.

Beck, I. L., McKeown, M. G., and Kucan, L. (2013). *Bringing words to life.* New York: Guilford.

Bigaj, J. (1968). *A reading program for gifted children in the primary grades.* ERIC Document Reproduction Service, ED 020086.

Blachowicz, C. L., Fisher, P. J., Ogle, D., and Watts-Taffe, S. (2006). Vocabulary: Questions from the classroom. *Reading Research Quarterly*, 41(4), 524–39.

Bond, C. W., and Bond, L. T. (1980). Reading instruction for the primary grade gifted student. *Georgia Journal of Reading*, 5, 33–36.

Bond, C. W., and Bond, L. T. (1983). Reading and the gifted student. *Roeper Review*, 5, 4–6.

Bradley, B. A., and Reinking, D. (2011). Enhancing research and practice in early childhood through formative and design experiments. *Early Childhood Development and Care*, 181(3), 305–19.

Briggs, C. J., Reis, S. M., and Sullivan, E. E. (2008). A national view of promising programs and practices for culturally, linguistically, and ethnically diverse gifted and talented students. *Gifted Child Quarterly*, 52(2), 131–45.

Burns, P., and Broman, B. (1983). *The language arts in childhood education.* Boston: Houghton-Mifflin.

Caraisco, J. (2007). Overcoming lethargy in gifted and talented education with contract activity packages: "I'm Choosing to Learn!" *Clearing House: A Journal of Educational Strategies, Issues and Ideas*, 80(6), 255–60.

Cashion, M., and Sullenger, K. (2000). "Contact us next year": Tracing teachers' use of gifted practices. *Roeper Review*, 23(1), 18.

Carr, D. (1984). The logic of intentional verbs. *Philosophical Investigations*, 7, 141–57. doi:10.1111/j.1467-9205.1984.tb00515.x.

Cassady, J., Cross, T., Dixon, F., and Williams, D. (Summer 2005). Effects of technology on critical thinking and essay writing among gifted adolescents. *Journal of Secondary Gifted Education*, 16 (4), 180–89.

Cassidy, J. (1981). Inquiry reading for the gifted. *Reading Teacher*, 35, 17–21.

Cazden, C., Cope, B., Fairclough, N., Gee, J. P., Kalantzis, M., Kress, G., et al. (The New London Group) (1996). A pedagogy of multiliteracies: designing social futures. *Harvard Educational Review*, 66(1), 60–92.

Chandler, K. (2001). Curriculum and instruction. In M. Landrum, C. Callahan, and B. Shaklee (Eds.), *Aiming for excellence: Annotations to the NAGC Pre K–Grade 12 gifted program standards* (53–65). Austin, TX: Prufrock.

Chiang, H. (2009). How accountability pressure on failing schools affects student achievement. *Journal of Public Economics*, 93, 1045–57.

Clarenbach, J. (February 2007). All gifted is local: Without federal guidance, no two districts deliver gifted education services in the same way. *School Administrator*, 64, 16–21.

Clark, B. (1983). *Growing up gifted: Developing the potential of children at home and at school.* Columbus: Merrill.

Colangelo, N. Assouline, S. G., and Gross, M. U. M. (2004). *A nation deceived: How schools hold back America's brightest students*, vol. 1. Iowa City, IA: The Connie Belin and Jacqueline N. Blank International Center for Gifted Education and Talent Development.

Cornett, C. E. (2011). *Creating meaning through literature and the arts: Arts integration for classroom teachers.* Fourth edition. Boston, MA: Allyn and Bacon.

Cramond, B., and Brodsky, R. (1996). Serving gifted students through inclusion in the heterogeneously grouped classroom. *Roeper Review*, 19(1), A-1.

Crocker, L., and Algina, J. (2008). *Introduction to classical and modern test theory*. Mason, OH: Cengage Learning.

DeVeaux, R. D., Velleman, P. F., and Bock, D. E. (2006). *Intro Stats*. Boston: Pearson Addison Wesley.

Dove, M., and Zitkovich, J. (2003). Technology driven group investigation for gifted elementary students. *Information Technology in Childhood Education*, 1, 223–41.

Duke, N. K., and Pearson, P. D. (2008/2009). Effective practices for developing reading comprehension. *Journal of Education*, 189(1/2), 107–22.

Durdu, P. O., Yalabik, N., and Cagiltay, K. (2009). A distributed online curriculum and courseware development model. *Educational Technology and Society*, 12(1), 230–48.

Durkin, D. (1966). *Children who read early*. New York: Teachers College Press.

Durkin, D. (1978). What classroom observations reveal about reading comprehension instruction. *Reading Research Quarterly*, 14(4), 481–533.

Dybdahl, C., Shaw, D., and Blahouse, E. (1997). The impact of computer on writing: No simple answers. *Computers in the Schools*, 13(3/4), 41–53.

Dymock, S. (2007). Comprehension strategy instruction: Teaching narrative text structure awareness. *Reading Teacher*, 61(2), 161–67.

Florida Department of Education. (2006). Florida State Rule: 6A-6.03019 Special Instructional Programs for Students Who Are Gifted. Retrieved from https://www.flrules.org/gateway/ruleNo.asp?ID=6A-6.03019.

Florida Department of Education. (2009). FCAT test design summary. Retrieved from http://fcat.fldoe.org/pdf/fc05designsummary.pdf.

Frezise, R. (1978). What about a reading program for the gifted? *Reading Teacher*, 31, 742–47.

Friedman, T. L. (2007). *The world is flat 3.0: A brief history of the twenty-first century*. New York: Picador.

Gall, M. D., Gall, J. P., and Borg, W. R. (2007). *Educational research: An introduction*. Eighth edition. Boston: Allyn and Bacon.

Gee, J. P. (2007). *What video games have to teach us about learning and literacy*. Second edition. New York: Palgrave MacMillan.

Gee, J. P. (2008). *Getting over the slump: Innovation strategies to promote children's learning*. New York: Joan Ganz Cooney Center at Sesame Workshop.

Gee, J. P. (2013). Games for learning. *Educational Horizons*, 91(4), 16–20.

Glass, G. V., and Hopkins, K. D. (1996). *Statistical methods in education and psychology*. Third edition. Needham Heights, MA: Allyn and Bacon.

Goodman, Y., Burke, C. and Sherman, B. (1980). *Reading strategies focus on comprehension*. New York: Holt, Rinehart and Winston.

Gross, M. (2006). *Tips for parents: What we know from longitudinal studies of E/PG children*. Davidson Institute for Talent Development.

Groves, R. M., Fowler, F. J, Jr., Couper, M. P., Lepkowski, J. M., Singer, E., and Tourangeau, R. (2009). *Survey methodology*. Second edition. Hoboken, NJ: John Wiley.

Gullat, D. E. (2008). Enhancing student learning through arts integration: Implications for the profession. *High School Journal*, 91(4), 12–25.

Gunning, T. (1992). *Creating reading instruction for all children*. Boston: Allyn and Bacon.

Harvey, S., and Goudvis, A. (2007). *Strategies that work*. Second edition. Portland, OR: Stenhouse.

Hollingworth, L. S. (1942). *Children above 180 IQ*. Yonkers-on-Hudson, NY: World Books.

Hoskisson, K., and Tompkins, G. (1987). *Language arts content and teaching strategies*. Columbus, OH: Merrill.

Howell, H. (1987). Language, literature and vocabulary development for gifted students. *Reading Teacher*, 40, 500–504.

International Reading Association. (2002). Integrating literacy and technology in the curriculum: A position statement of the International Reading Association. Newark, DE: International Reading Association.

Jenkins, H., Clinton, K., Purushotma, R., Robison, A. J., and Weigel, M. (2005). *Confronting the challenges of participatory culture: Media education for the 21st century*. MacArthur

Foundation. Retrieved from http://www.newmedialiteracies.org/wp-content/uploads/pdfs/ NMLWhitePaper.pdf.

Karnes, M., and Johnson, L. (1987). Educating young gifted/talented: An imperative. *Journal for the Education of the Gifted*, 10, 195–215.

Lam, T. C. M., and Klockars, A. J. (1982). Anchor point effects on the equivalence of question-naire items. *Journal of Educational Measurement*, 19, 317–22.

Lankshear, C., and Knobel, M. (2007). Sampling "the new" in new literacies. In M. Knobel and C. Lankshear (Eds.), *A New Literacies Sampler* (1–23). New York: Peter Lang.

Law, C., and Kaufhold, J. A. (2009). An analysis of the use of critical thinking skills in Reading and Language Arts instruction. *Reading Improvement*, 46(1), 29–34.

Levande, D. (1999). Gifted readers and reading instruction. *CAG Communicator*, 30(1).

Loveless, T., Parkas, S., and Duffett, A. (2008). *High-achieving students in the era of NCLB*. Washington, DC: Thomas B. Fordham Foundation and Institute.

Marland, S. P., Jr. (1972). *Education of the gifted and talented*. Report to the Congress of the United States by the Commissioner of Education. Washington, DC.

Mason, J. and Au, K. (1990). *Reading instruction for today*. New York: HarperCollins.

Ming, K. (2012). 10 content-area literacy strategies for art, mathematics, music, and physical education. *The Clearing House*, 85, 213–20.

Mistler-Jackson, M., and Songer, N. (2000). Student motivation and Internet technology: Are students empowered to learn science? *Journal of Research in Science Teaching*, 37(5), 459–79.

Mitchell, B. (1982). An update on the state of gifted education in the U.S. *Phi Delta Kappan*, 63, 357–58.

Nagy, W. E. and Scott, J. A. (2000). Vocabulary processes. In M. L. Kamil, P. B. Mosenthal, P. D. Pearson, and R. Barr (Eds.), *The handbook of reading research* (3: 269–84). Mahwah, NJ: Erlbaum.

National Association of Gifted Children. (2008a). What is giftedness? Retrieved from http://www.nagc.org/index.aspx?id=574.

National Association of Gifted Children. (2008b). Common characteristics. Retrieved from https://www.nagc.org/resources-publications/resources/my-child-gifted/commoncharacter-istics-gifted-individuals.

National Association of Gifted Children. (2013). 2012–2013 State of the states in gifted education: National policy and practice data. Washington, DC.

National Council of Teachers of Mathematics. (2000). *Principles and standards for school mathematics*. Reston, VA: NCTM. Retrieved from http://standards.nctm.org/document/chapter3/index.htm.

National Science Teachers Association. (2010). National Science Education Standards. Retrieved from http://www.nsta.org/publications/nses.aspx.

New Media Consortium. (2005). *A Global Imperative: The Report of the 21st Century Literacy Summit*. Austin, TX: New Media Consortium. Retrieved from http://www.nmc.org/pdf/Global_Imperative.pdf.

Parks, S. (2009). Teaching analytical and critical thinking skills in gifted education. In F. Karnes and S. Bean (Eds.), *Methods and materials for teaching the gifted*, third edition (261–300). Waco, TX: Prufrock.

Polette, N. (1984). *The research book for gifted programs, K–8*. Dayton, OH: Pieces of Learning.

Purcell, J. H., Burns, D. E., Tomlinson, C. A., Imbeau, M. B., and Martin, J. L. (2002). Bridging the gap: A tool and technique to analyze and evaluate gifted education curricular units. *Gifted Child Quarterly*, 46(4), 306–21.

Rabkin, N., and Redmond, R. (2006). The arts make a difference. *Educational Leadership*, 63(5), 60–64.

Rash, P. K., and Miller, A. D. (2000). A survey of practices of teachers of the gifted. *Roeper Review*, 22(3), 192–94.

Reback, R. (2008). Teaching to the rating: School accountability and the distribution of student achievement. *Journal of Public Economics*, 92, 1394–1415.

Reinking, D., and Bradley, B. A. (2008). *On formative and design experiments: Approaches to language and literacy research.* New York: Teachers College Press.

Reis, S. M. (2007). *Research-based practices for talented readers.* Pearson/Scott Foresman Research Brief.

Reis, S. M., Eckert, R. D., Schreiber, F. J., Jacobs, J. K., Briggs, C., Gubbins, E. J., et al. (2005). *The schoolwide enrichment model reading study.* Research Monograph 05214. Storrs: National Research Center on the Gifted and Talented, University of Connecticut.

Reis, S. M., and Renzulli, J. S. (2009). Myth 1: The gifted and talented constitute one single homogeneous group and giftedness is a way of being that stays in the person over time and experiences. *Gifted Child Quarterly,* 53(4), 233–35.

Reis, S. M., and Renzulli, J. S. (2010). Is there still a need for gifted education? An examination of current research. *Learning and Individual Differences,* 20(4), 308–17.

Renzulli, J. (1977). *The enrichment triad model: Guide for developing defensible programs for the gifted and talented.* Mansfield Center, CT: Creative Learning.

Renzulli, J. (1988). The multiple menu model for developing differentiated curriculum for the gifted and talented. *Gifted Child Quarterly,* 32, 298–309.

Renzulli, J. S. (2005). The three-ring conception of giftedness: A developmental model for creative productivity. In R. J. Sternberg and J. E. Davidson (Eds.), *Conceptions of giftedness* (53–92). Cambridge: Cambridge University Press.

Renzulli, J. S., Smith, L. H., White, A. J., Callahan, C. M., Hartman, R. K., and Westberg, K. L. (2002). *Scales for rating the behavioral characteristics of superior students.* Revised edition. Mansfield Center, CT: Creative Learning.

Ries, E. (2011). *The lean startup.* New York: Crown Business.

Riley, T.L. (2009). Teaching gifted and talented students in regular classrooms. In F. Karnes and S. Bean (Eds.), *Methods and materials for teaching the gifted,* third edition (631–72). Waco, TX: Prufrock.

Roblyer, M. D., and Doering, A. H. (2010). *Integrating educational technology into teaching.* Fifth edition. Boston: Allyn and Bacon.

Roser, N. L., and Martinez, M. G. (Eds.). (2005). *What a character! Character study as a guide to literary meaning making in grades K–8.* Newark, DE: International Reading Association.

Rupley, W. (1984). Reading teacher effectiveness: Implications for teaching the gifted. *Roeper Review,* 7, 70–72.

Sakiey, E. (1980). *Reading for the gifted.* ERIC Document Reproduction Service ED186881.

Schwartz, L. (1984). *Exceptional students in the mainstream.* Belmont, CA: Wadsworth.

Shaffer, D., and Gee, J. P. (2005). Before every child is left behind: How epistemic games can solve the coming crisis in education. Paper retrieved from http://www.academiccolab.org/resources/documents/learning_crisis.pdf.

Shaughnessy, M. (1994). *Gifted and reading.* Paper presented at the annual meeting of the International Reading Association, San Antonio, TX.

Shaunessy-Dedrick, E., Evans, L., Ferron, J., and Lindo, M. (2015). Effects of differentiated reading on elementary students' reading comprehension and attitudes toward reading. *Gifted Child Quarterly,* 59(2), 91–107.

Sternberg, R. J. (1982). Lies we live by: Misapplication of tests in identifying the gifted. *Gifted Child Quarterly,* 26(4), 157–61.

Sternberg, R. J. (1987). Most vocabulary is learned from context. In M. G. McKeown and M. E. Curtis (Eds.), *The nature of vocabulary acquisition* (89–106). Hillsdale, NJ: Erlbaum.

Sternberg, R. J., Ferrari, M., Clinkenbeard, P., and Grigorenko, E. L. (1996). Identification, instruction, and assessment of gifted children: A construct validation of a Triarchic Model. *Gifted Child Quarterly,* 40, 129–37.

Sternberg, R. J., and Zhang, L. (1995). What do we mean by giftedness? A pentagonal implicit theory. *Gifted Child Quarterly,* 39(2), 88–94.

Swaby, B. (1982). The A.I.M.E.: A classroom model for the reading instruction of gifted readers. *Indiana Reading Quarterly,* 35(8), 270–77.

Teale, W. (1982). Learning to read and write naturally. *Language Arts,* 59, 555–570.

Terman, L. (1925). Mental and physical traits of a thousand gifted children. In L. Terman (Ed.), *Genetic studies of genius,* vol. 1. Stanford, CA: Stanford University Press.

Tomlinson, C. A. (2005). Quality curriculum and instruction for highly able students. *Theory into Practice*, 44(2), 160–66.

Trevise, R. (1984). Teaching reading to the gifted. In A. Harris and E. Sipay (Eds.), *Reading on reading instruction.* New York: Longman.

Tuttle, F. B., Becker, L. A., and Sousa, J. A. (1988). *Characteristics and identification of gifted and talented students.* Third edition. Washington, DC: National Education Association.

U.S. Department of Education, Office of Educational Research and Improvement (1993). *National excellence: A case for developing America's talent.* Washington, DC: U.S. Government Printing Office.

Vacca, J., Vacca, R., and Gove, M. (1991). *Reading and learning to read.* New York: Harper-Collins.

Van den Akker, J., Gravemeijer, K., McKenney, S., and Nieveen, N. (Eds.). (2006). *Educational design research.* London: Routledge.

VanTasssel-Baska, J. (2013). Curriculum for the gifted: A commitment to excellence. *Gifted Child Today*, 36(3), 213–15.

VanTassel-Baska J., and Brown, E. F. (2007). An analysis of the efficacy of curriculum models in gifted education. *Gifted Child Quarterly*, 51(4), 342–58.

VanTassel-Baska, J., and Brown, E. F. (2009). An analysis of gifted education curriculum models. In F. Karnes and S. Bean (Eds.), *Methods and materials for teaching the gifted*, third edition (75–106). Waco, TX: Prufrock.

VanTassel-Baska, J., and Stambaugh, T. (2005). Challenges and possibilities for serving gifted learners in the regular classroom. *Theory into Practice*, 44, 211–17.

VanTassel-Baska, J., and Stambaugh, T. (2006). *Comprehensive curriculum for gifted learners.* Third edition. Needham Heights, MA: Allyn and Bacon.

VanTassel-Baska, J., and Stambaugh, T. (2009). *What works: 20 years of curriculum development and research for advanced learners, 1988–2008* (Report). Center for Gifted Education, College of William and Mary. Retrieved from http://education.wm.edu/centers/cfge/curriculum/documents/WhatWorks.pdf.

VanTassel-Baska, J., and Wood, S. (2010). The Integrated Curriculum Model (ICM). *Learning and Individual Differences*, 20, 345–57.

Wallace, R. M. (2004). A framework for understanding teaching with the internet. *American Educational Research Journal*, 41(2), 447–85.

Wallen, C. (1974). Fostering reading growth for gifted and creative readers at the primary level. In M. Labuda (Ed.), *Creative reading for gifted learners: A design for excellence.* Newark, DE: I.R.A.

Watters, J. J., and Diezmann, C. M. (1997). Optimising activities to meet the needs of young children gifted in mathematics and science. In P. Rillero and J. Allison (Eds.), *Creative Childhood Experiences in Mathematics and Science* (143–70). Projects, Activity Series, and Centers for Early Childhood. ERIC Clearinghouse for Science, Mathematics, and Environmental Education, Columbus, OH.

Witty, P. (1981). *Reading for the gifted and creative student.* Newark, DE: I.R.A.

Witty, P. (1985). Rationale for fostering creative reading in the gifted and creative. In M. Labuda (Ed.), *Creative learning for gifted learners*, second edition. Newark, DE: I.R.A.

Wood, P. F. (2008). Reading instruction with gifted and talented readers: A series of unfortunate events or a sequence of auspicious results? *Gifted Child Today*, 31(3), 16–26.

Zinser, R., and Poledink, P. (Fall 2005). The Ford Partnership for Advanced Studies: A new case for curriculum integration in technology education. *Journal of Technology Education*, 17, 69–82.

II

Culturally Relevant Pedagogy and
Marginalized Students

Chapter Four

Culturally Responsible Teaching

An Example and Lessons Learned

Megan Adams

Introduction Classroom Example: Mrs. Gaines

When Mrs. Gaines began teaching in a rural, Title I school in the southeastern United States, she decided to approach the racial tensions she noticed head on. Mrs. Gaines heard phrases like "conflict," "stirring up," "unrest," and "fight back" in her first teaching context. Despite inequalities evident in local education outcomes in the new teaching context, Mrs. Gaines was not hearing those phrases from teachers, students, or community members. Instead, there seemed an acceptance of the inequalities.

Despite a population roughly half African American and half Caucasian, African American students were nearly three times less likely to graduate from high school. How did the community feel about the inequity? How could this be an achievement gap if the school did not provide equal opportunity? Those questions were not asked in her presence. She began questioning within the silences.

Her classroom became a place where true scenarios, from history or the media, could be questioned and debated through literature. She learned that for many of the African American students, this was not a typical experience in their education. She noticed more of her students coming to her room at times of the day when they weren't in her class.

Her classroom became "a home base." In retrospect, she notes, she could have guessed what was going to happen by the reactions of several adults, as there was not universal agreement that her approach was appropriate. Adult reactions ranged from excitement because "it wasn't being done prior" to distrust that she was "causing trouble" to fear over possible consequences.

Over the course of the unit investigated in this chapter, she started noticing something from the students in her classes. The students who were not of color were retreating from her. During a presentation by a group of students,

*she told a cluster of boys to be quiet. "She hates us because we are white,"
they whispered.*

*She was prepared for classroom debates to get heated; she had prepared a
protocol for students to discuss tensions in class; she had prepared her principal by explaining that this unit was going to incite uncomfortable conversation. She was prepared for students to reject the conversations she was proposing; she was—she admits stupidly—taken by surprise when students were
passive aggressive and openly showing racism. She says that while she did not
handle the comment with grace, she did end class that day insisting that
everyone in the room question their own assumptions.*

*The reaction from students in the room at the time was typical. Students
were confused, upset, and angry that she was upset. The discussion in the
following days about the text ranged as it had before. What was unusual was
this: at the end of that day, an African American student who was in a different
grade and different section of her class came to her in the hallway. He asked if
she was OK. The student was visibly angry as he nodded and said, "I don't
know why we couldn't have just one who was ours." The silence that had
troubled her at the beginning of the year was beginning to change.*

INCORPORATING CULTURALLY RESPONSIBLE TEACHING

This chapter highlights a lesson that could have been a useful tool for tack-
ling some problems in a specific school climate. The practitioner focus emphasizes the narratives of students collected by the teacher as she integrated a
lesson that challenged the norms of a small, rural, southern town. The chapter
also underscores what teachers must do to incorporate culturally responsible
teaching in a way that is fair to all children; children should not feel further
marginalized, as the African American students were in Mrs. Gaines's vignette above. While the black students were visiting Mrs. Gaines's room and
feeling empowered in some spaces in the school, the underlying racism(s) of
the white students was becoming more visible.

The reflexive practice necessary to deliver and modify a unit can allow
teachers to become stronger practitioners. Graduate students, preservice
teachers, and younger teachers should remember that social justice must be
incorporated into teaching even when it is uncomfortable—especially when
it is uncomfortable—or the students will not know how to collaborate in the
world beyond public schooling.

A POSSIBLE CLASSROOM PEDAGOGY: MRS. GAINES'S
CONTEXT

Mrs. Gaines's introduction to teaching came in a rural, Title I school whose
population was composed of nearly all African American students. During
her first few years as a language arts teacher there, she says she learned a

great deal through formal and informal study of her students. The students had very developed affinity identities, but less developed academic identities (Gee, 2000–2001).

She began changing her practice so that she spent a great deal of time developing a sense of community within her classroom. This was not a new idea, particularly as a tool to engage marginalized youth, yet it was new to her practice (Anyon, 1980; Delpit, 1992). In doing so, she noticed a major improvement in the effort of her students, which led directly to their increased performance.

When she began teaching in a different rural school, Mrs. Gaines brought with her a greater confidence in building community as a tool to engage marginalized youth. During the first year at the new school, she did some research. Within the group of third-year students—not referred to as juniors because many were behind on credits—there was disparity between the performance of Caucasian and African American students. Among the African American population, 36 percent were behind on credits as a result of failing courses, while that was true of only 9 percent of white students.

This spurred her to put together a discussion group to talk about what was hindering student performance. She began changes to her curriculum in a strangely conventional way in high schools in the rural South; she began with a unit on *The Adventures of Huckleberry Finn*. The novel was chosen intentionally because it is complex reading and appropriate for American literature, but it also has a lower readability level and allows for rich discussion about race.

Mrs. Gaines was pleased with the engagement of all of her students. While Jim is a problematic character, discussing the way he is treated in the novel (childlike, subservient to Huck) allowed the students to draw parallels to the class structure visible in the school and community. Mrs. Gaines wanted to emphasize those tensions and problematize Jim further in order to allow for debate and rich conversation to begin in the classroom.

The goal, she says, was for students to question the norms many of them had accepted in their community. She began a study group after school in order to assist students who struggled in class and to ask them for feedback about various lessons. Those discussions contributed a great deal to the lesson she delivered on Huck Finn and racial tension. The cyclical process of delivering instruction, discussing school issues (and issues in the United States), and reflecting on that process was incredibly powerful.

She found that insisting on themes and certain anchor texts while offering reading choice to meet other standards allowed the creativity and sense of community in her classroom to grow. While cultivating a successful classroom environment was never as easy as in the community where students had stronger identities outside of school, she found that many of her marginalized students slowly began to thrive.

CONNECTING TO THE STANDARDS

When this lesson was planned, the team in the English department at Mrs. Gaines's school was using the Common Core Standards and worked with their local regional education support agency (RESA) to roll out the Common Core Georgia Performance Standards. The specificity required in the grade level bands is problematic for students like those in this class; Mrs. Gaines describes the difficulty in choosing anchor texts that did not make students reading below grade level feel disenfranchised.

In the grade 9 and 10 level bands for literature, standard CCSS.ELA-Literacy.RL.9–10.7 reads, "Analyze the representation of a subject or a key scene in two different artistic mediums, including what is emphasized or absent in each treatment (e.g., Auden's "Musee des Beaux Arts" and Breughel's *Landscape with the Fall of Icarus*)." (corestandards.org). However, according to the Lexile Analyzer (www.lexile.com), Auden's text is at a Lexile level of 1170.

That band is appropriate for readers who are on grade level. What about those who are not? Based on the data from the End of Course Test and Criterion Referenced Competency Test scores, the students in Mrs. Gaines's class fell into the fourth- and fifth-grade Lexile band, which meant that they needed texts in the 740–1010 range (www.lexile.com). Heibert and Mesmer (2013) explored the far-reaching impact of increasing text complexity requirements; their study explores what may happen when increasing the complexity of the second- and third-grade level bands. They are concerned about students who are still near that second- or third-grade level band and yet have made it to middle school or high school. Will they be able to achieve the Carnegie units necessary to graduate? Will they be able to pass the tests necessary to graduate?

Mrs. Gaines felt sure of one thing: in order for students to take the assignments seriously and put forth effort, they needed to believe they could accomplish the tasks. Thus, the anchor text became *Huck Finn*, and supplemental informational texts were newspaper articles and research articles on race and on Twain's portrayal of characters and southern life.

REACHING ALL STUDENTS: A SAMPLE LESSON

"The study of short texts is particularly useful. . . . The Common Core State Standards place high priority on the close, sustained reading of complex text. . . . Such reading focuses on what lies within the four corners of the text" (Coleman and Pimentel, 2012). Many educators and professionals who work with marginalized youth know that emphasizing relevance is crucial in encouraging reluctant readers to improve their reading.

More importantly, educators must encourage readers performing below grade level to foster a love of reading (Hatt, 2007; Heron-Hruby et al., 2008). If students may only use the "four corners of the text" (Coleman and Pimentel, 2012), how will their teachers help them build the background knowledge needed to approach such complex texts with confidence (Alvermann, 2002)?

The Adventures of Huckleberry Finn can be the backdrop of many important lessons involving critical literacy. Previously, Mrs. Gaines describes using Ernest Gaines's *A Lesson before Dying* or *A Gathering of Old Men* as anchor texts. While the Lexile levels are comparable to the demands of *Huck Finn*, the vocabulary demands and comprehension requirements are less vigorous.

Mrs. Gaines decided to offer several challenging texts as optional reading in the unit paired with several texts by Walter Dean Myers for readers performing at a lower level. *Huck Finn* was chosen because it offers problematic portrayals, uses antiquated language and mindsets, and should be questioned as a text furthering racism (Carey-Webb, 1993, 2001; Henry, 1992). Mrs. Gaines was influenced by a PBS lesson plan and curriculum developed for teachers wanting to criticize the text and teach it in context (*Huck Finn in context*, n.d.).

The unit Mrs. Gaines taught explored the anchor text while students read supplemental informational and fictional texts. Much of the work was based on student choice; group-led presentations on topics of interest, individual reflections, and reports were all important assessments used during the unit. Students could choose to explore the "n word debate" (Winfrey, 2009), the controversy on Twain as a reporter (Just, 2010), race portrayals in historical texts (Perkins, 2009), or their own topic with teacher approval.

The result was a text-rich unit in which students explored a controversy that was very real in their lives inside and outside of school; Mrs. Gaines heard frequently that the assignments were being discussed widely in the community. The discussion group that met after school also gave Mrs. Gaines insight into the lesson and how students were feeling about the work. The group met once per month and was targeted to students who needed additional support and were more than five credits behind toward graduation.

BACKGROUND INFORMATION ON STUDENTS

In the discussion group informing the teaching of the *Huck Finn* unit, students were not feeling empowered, an experience that was similar across the students, though the ways the students dealt with that feeling of inadequacy and lack of control were different. All four students are African American males, ranging in age from fifteen to seventeen. Three of the students were third-year students, and one was a second-year student.

Bodie and Ralph both felt that there were things they could do differently to change the way their teachers felt about them. Yet both of them felt that their teachers did not like them and thus had little time to help them. Ace and Jimmy also felt their teachers didn't like them; however, they had become more hardened by that perception. Ace and Jimmy were openly defiant because they felt that it was too late for them to be well-liked, and they felt that without being well-liked or "one of them honors kids," they would not be receiving any help from their teachers.

What would happen if they did not get help? Ralph and Bodie said that without help they would never graduate with their classmates, and Ace and Jimmy said they would drop out because there was no point in continuing to attempt tests they were not able to pass. Jimmy was frequently in trouble in school for disrespect. This was often seen in his use of profanity in the classroom.

Being out of class either to serve in-school suspension or other forms of suspension kept him from performing in class and led to a pattern: Jimmy did not earn very many credits each semester and was thus two years behind in school already. He said, "If I say anything to a teacher, they get a smart mouth. Then I get another write up. The teachers don't understand if I got a smart mouth it is only because I'm so frustrated. I ain't in ninth grade no more. And I can't do that stuff on the computer. It is too hard and nobody can help me."

The work on the computer was the school's credit recovery system, which of course he needed in order to catch up with other third-year students. However, he had not had any success on that program either. Yet Jimmy still saw college as an option, and he did not understand exactly what was required for the field he wanted to be part of.

"Well, you don't really have to go to college . . . I don't think so . . . to get your CDL. I mean, I might need the mechanic part, so I can fix [the truck] if it breaks down." As shown by his lack of success, there was not a possibility of increasing the rigor for Jimmy yet. What were the teachers to do? Neither the school nor the district had answers for effectively differentiating at this scale.

Ace said that going on for more schooling after high school would be pointless for Jimmy. "We are going to be partners. Jimmy can't do the business stuff and doesn't need to be going to school. We want to own a business together." Ace was very sure about the path he wanted to take after high school. He wanted to earn his credits in order to attend a two-year school for business and then own a trucking company with Jimmy where they would be owner-operators.

Yet Ace felt very bitter about his teachers' lack of attention. He said, "Sometimes I want to tell the teacher what I think of him. Who he think he is? But it is a game you gotta play. Either you have the power to stay in Crossroads [alternative school] or the power to get run over by the principal." He was frustrated that teachers were not treating them like young adults. "We need to be able to speak our mind at school, and ain't no teacher gonna let me do that." Ace often shut down when pushed to answer questions, and it was clear that the attention of the teachers was actually very important to him. While Jimmy openly acted out, Ace held his anger in. He acted indifferent to school and to teachers as a defense mechanism.

With appropriate support, Ace could easily have performed the writing included in the anchor standards. He has natural intelligence and a lot of "street smarts." However, he would need a great deal of scaffolding to read and write at grade level, and, additionally, a classroom community would be imperative to get through the shield he has put up. All four of the students have learned to put up a shield in various forms.

Bodie's shield was being the class clown. Bodie said, "It is hard to concentrate if you don't get it," and "the teacher doesn't explain it in a way I understand." When he didn't understand and became bored in class, his habit was to talk to other students and act out. He said that this has created a cycle. "I mean, I like the teachers. But it is a real problem if you got tardies or something and you get ISS [in-school suspension]. Or maybe I play and get it. But then you don't get your work down there and you get even farther behind."

His primary concern was that each year the work in his classes was becoming more difficult, but he was never able to do the work the year before. Thus, though he was progressing through the levels, he wasn't succeeding at each level and was missing the needed foundation. This seemed to go back to grade school. He emphasized that "the work is too hard to do on my own, and there is too much, and I just can't get it or see the end of it." Clearly, Bodie needs a great deal of help before performing at the increased rigor required by the Common Core exemplars (www.corestandards.org). However, he was already behind in school. When would he have time to receive the additional help and support he needed while keeping up with the demands of his courses?

Ralph did not agree with giving up on the chance for success. "If a teacher doesn't have time for me, I find someone else." He understood the cycle Bodie mentions but said that it was his fault he hadn't found another time to go see the teacher. He said, "I was on the teacher's good side, but then others were talking and I started playing around a lot, so now I'm trying to work my way back in."

Ralph was unique to this group in part because he had a very supportive family. Many of his conversations were about the demands of his parents and his sisters. He was also unique in that he never placed blame on any teacher in the school. He felt strongly that students needed to find teachers they were able to work with and that the motivating force in student achievement was the student himself or herself.

When asked about problems that could come up that were contrary to Ralph's opinion, the students agreed that sometimes things were beyond student control. For example, what happens if the teacher does not like you? All four agreed, "If the teacher don't like you, there ain't no way you are going to pass. All of us know that." Ralph said he had one teacher who "gives him control of his grade" by allowing him to make up missed work. If perception is reality, are any of these students going to go see a teacher they believe dislikes them—a teacher who possibly does not know that the students feel this way?

As teachers, how can we know when a student starts feeling it is "too late"? Are there ways to avoid the cycle the four students speak of? In addition, how can we move to the Common Core without a very clear plan for supporting students who are not on grade level before we develop the tests?

WHAT DID THE STUDENTS SEE HAPPENING?

The first assertion made by the students was that the teacher and the marginalized youth did not share power. Their view was that the teacher had the most power—and, if it was shared, it was only shared with the "smart" or "honors" or "good" students. In studying *Huck Finn*, they felt that the treatment of Jim as a "dummy" was not so different from how they were treated at school.

Mrs. Gaines expressed her fear that they were not able to criticize the text enough because they saw the treatment as something that had not changed. In the discussion group, she asked the students how they could be part of a change to better the school and community.

The students wanted to address the inequity. Students perceived a difference in the treatment of those who shared power with the teacher and those who did not (Apple, 1986; Clark, 1991; Ogbu, 1987). Again, this is commonly mentioned as a cause of social stratification among marginalized youth (Ogbu, 1992; Ream and Palardy, 2008). Why is this significant? In order for students to meet the goals of the preamble to the Common Core, they must be "prepared for success upon graduating high school" (www.corestandards.org).

This presumes that students will be able to graduate from high school. In this focus group, the lack of perceived belonging in the school was part of what was keeping students from attaining grade-level achievement. Another part of the students' lack of success—as measured by Carnegie units earned—was increasing rigor without adequate support. Units like this one, incorporating a wide variety of text demands while emphasizing critical thinking and cultural relevance, might be one way to engage students in this situation.

Bishop (2012) described identity as the factor that could keep students from becoming a different self in school. The identity taken on by students in school can directly determine how successful the students become. Students should be able to "become a different person with respect to the norms, practices, and modes of interactions determined by one's learning environment" (Bishop, 2012, p. 36). Most importantly for teachers and teacher researchers, part of the way those students form their school identities is through their interactions with teachers (Markus and Nurius, 1986).

If students are not developing their various identities, are they ready to meet the expectations of college and work, as expressly outlined in the preamble to the Common Core (corestandards.org; edweek.org)? Are we helping marginalized students understand not only the content but also the characteristics of successful employees and college students? The answer for the students in this group is no, we are not.

If we as teachers allow the classroom to become a community where all stakeholders are equal partners, we immediately increase the possible success of our marginalized students. We also put them in a position of controlling their own academic success instead of seeing an other as the root of the problem, as so many of the boys in this discussion group did. Ogbu argues that the problems affecting the social adjustment and academic success of black students are cultural problems that span the classroom, school, society, and community of those students (1992, p. 288–89).

Ogbu suggests that if a student's community positively promotes education and its values, then the student is more likely to succeed. In addition, the more positive communities the student is a part of, the more likely the student is to value the cultural capital provided by school. This suggests that the investment needed to create a classroom community that is a safe space for all students to share and learn is worth it.

In part, these students, who do not perceive control over their academic lives, could be provided greater control if more helpful feedback were provided to them in the classroom; this phenomenon has been noted in other studies (Cassidy et al., 2003). Adolescents actively seek certain types of feedback and will accept negative feedback over no feedback at all (p. 612).

There has been "little empirical examination of the active role children and adolescents may play in selecting the information about themselves that they receive" (p. 612); however, adolescents "tend to re-create familiar social environments as part of an attempt to maintain coherence of the self" (p.

613). The students in this discussion group were certainly describing this process.

The cycle of frustration due to lack of understanding, acting out, reprimand, and punishment was discussed in detail in many of our sessions. Yet the students did not seem to know any other way to participate in their academic community. Had they been taught another way? Were their teachers fostering a positive community for marginalized youth? Most of the boys were not perceiving it that way, if it was in fact happening in the school.

How does that tie to the lesson? After the lesson that was described as "successful on the surface," Mrs. Gaines modified the way that her community addressed larger, more difficult issues. When racial tension exists in the school, why not discuss that tension as the community reads about racial tensions in a book? The next time the lesson was delivered in her new school, Mrs. Gaines decided to be braver than she had been in that initial lesson. She did not connect local tensions or issues in the media to tensions in the texts; she allowed students to draw those parallels.

However, in describing and exploring the themes of each unit while activating prior knowledge, Mrs. Gaines decided to insist that those themes be prevalent issues in the community. These included working with the administrators in the building, working with the juvenile justice officers on local issues, and watching the news channels the students recommended.

WHAT MIGHT BE DONE?

Teachers need to "spell out the cultural assumptions on which the classroom (and schooling) operate" (Osborne, 1996, p. 298). In this example, many of the students in the discussion group described how isolated they felt in their school. They described not being able to even hope for college because they were told they were ineligible to register for foreign-language classes in their school. Should the school have let them believe that they were mistaken? Was Mrs. Gaines risking further anger by agreeing with and confirming their beliefs?

Advocacy is one of the most important components in working in a school with a large marginalized population (Athanases and Martin, 2006; Green, McCollum, and Hays, 2008). As teachers create lessons that promote conversations about social justice, they must be willing to take those conversations outside of the classroom in order to act as agents of change more broadly. Perhaps most importantly, during any of these changes teachers must be aware of the needs of marginalized youth in their classrooms.

A combination of warmth and rigor shows students that teachers expect them to perform well and that they care about their success (Osborne, 1996). Often, teachers misunderstand what students need to be successful because of the time spent by administrators training teachers to analyze numbers instead of people (1996). Instead, focusing on individuals and delving into what is hindering their success will lead to the best outcomes.

Schools with populations that are racially and socioeconomically diverse should include professional development for teachers on the unique needs of marginalized youth (Bailey, 2003). Workshops on testing and differentiation are only helpful if teachers are taught about their particular students.

In the specific case of this lesson, there are several things that could have been done. At the end of each lesson, Mrs. Gaines should have been asking pointed questions and collecting journal entries. She should have created a classroom blog to take the pulse of all of her students, and she should have been journaling herself.

As she looked over the data—or ideally used a teacher learning community to read over the data—she would find herself making assumptions. Reflexive journaling, in particular within learning communities, can allow teachers to realize what adjustments might be made more quickly than waiting for concrete student feedback at the end of a unit.

What would this mean for teaching a controversial novel today? You would not have time to conduct a critical discourse analysis after each class session. However, you could quickly write your thoughts, perceptions, and student quotes in your journal to review later. You could redesign the daily discussions as needed, based on what you saw after writing in a reflexive journal each afternoon.

When you noticed that you overlooked a comment that a student made or failed to address a concern brought up in your third-period class, you could begin the discussion there the following day. These quick practices would allow for more voices to be heard in your classroom; culturally responsible teaching could become a habit and a goal to work for as a classroom community.

IMPLICATIONS

Experts do not agree that implementing the changes above will directly impact positive changes in student achievement. In fact, several studies on interventions conducted with students performing below reading level and needing Response to Intervention help in middle and high school have shown few gains for those students (Fletcher et al., 2007; Kamil et al., 2008). Other research notes that if students are able to change their self-perceptions as readers, they are able to make far more significant improvements (O'Brien, Beach, and Scharber, 2007).

If that research proves true, teachers and schools could use the shift to Common Core standards as an opportunity to improve the interventions necessary for struggling students—and important gains may be made. However, far more disturbing are the data showing that students who are not yet ready for high school, are below grade level in reading, and are not able to successfully complete high-school level work—which is increasing in difficulty as the Common Core is implemented—are more likely to drop out as early as ninth grade (McCallumore and Sparapani, 2010; Neild, Stoner-Eby, and Furstenberg, 2008).

The contradictory options for addressing the needs of marginalized youth—and, in this case, all students—and the obstacles in public schools for doing so create the opportunity for discussion and growth about how communities may be reformed. Community cannot just take place in a classroom or school; it must take place at all levels (Bailey, 2003; Kahne and Bailey, 1999; Plucker, 1998). Deryl Bailey said that "improving economic and social conditions for a community or particular group in the United States has always been linked to education" (2003, p. 15).

Instead of rallies like those being held at the state capital in Georgia (Downey, 2014), perhaps citizens, policy makers, educators, and students could meet to have honest conversations about what is needed in classrooms and what we could do to improve implementation and assessment.

CONCLUSION

In thinking through Mrs. Gaines's *Huck Finn* lesson, there are several conclusions that may be drawn. The text was appropriate according to the anchor standard for reading literature. Additionally, the text allowed her to address critical literacy and many of the standards for reading for information. Students learned while working on their culminating activity about the life and times of Mark Twain. What she was missing was a multifaceted approach.

Students needed to feel that their voices were being heard not only by their teacher but also by their peers. There should have been multiple platforms for communication in order to minimize discomfort and maximize student participation. From the beginning, a classroom community was being established. However, the tensions in that community often shut down lines of thought that could have blossomed to real student growth.

Mrs. Gaines should have taken that important work further by giving students an online platform; classroom blogs are well-researched tools allowing students more freedom to express ideas they might find too difficult to discuss in class (Jones and Holland, 2013; Mostafa, 2014). Students would also have the opportunity to digest information that ran counter to their internal narratives; a blog would allow them to take time outside of class to decide how to respond when unpacking their own biases.

Furthermore, Mrs. Gaines should have begun her own reflexivity journal from the first day of the lesson. She would then have had the opportunity to make minor adjustments throughout the lesson to ensure that groups were not feeling further alienated as they read the text and worked on projects. While many of her students were below the required Lexile level for *Huck Finn* to be appropriate, they were able to read it and participate because of the scaffolding provided.

Perhaps this is another way to address some inequities extant in the current form of Common Core. Students used discussions and read-aloud practice as entry points into a difficult text; they then used their own opinions and experiences to address the relevance of the text to their own lives. Instead of choosing alternate texts for students performing below grade level in reading, allowing all students to use the same text in different ways might be preferable.

That would have made this a stronger lesson and also would have addressed more of the important components of the standards. It would have been a way to use new literacies in the classroom, allowing students the opportunity to engage with an older text in a more meaningful way (Knobel and Lankshear, 2007; Gee, 2003). Most importantly, the classroom community might have grown closer if she had approached diversity as needed rather than imposing an agenda for changing how the students handled diversity.

That difference in mindset might have taken longer to show results; it also might have given students more of the tools they needed to make those changes last outside of that single classroom. As teachers new to incorporating culturally responsible teaching look into changes in curriculum (such as Common Core) that could allow them to do so effectively, they should consider their students' voices—and silence—in every step of that process.

REFERENCES

Adams, M. G. (2012). A phenomenological study of adolescents' perceptions of empowerment Doctoral dissertation, University of Georgia, Athens, Georgia.

Alvermann, D. E. (2002). Effective literacy instruction for adolescents. *Journal of Literacy Research*, 34, 189–208.

Anyon, J. (1980). Social class and the hidden curriculum of work. *Journal of Education*, 162, 67–92.

Apple, M. J. (1986). *Teachers and texts: A political economy of class and gender relations in education.* London: Routledge and Kegan Paul.

Athanases, S. Z., and Martin, K. J. (2006). Learning to advocate for educational equity in a teacher credential program. *Teaching and Teacher Education*, 22(6), 627–46.

Bailey, D. F. (2003). PGOTM: Creating a pipeline of African American male scholars. *Journal of Men's Studies*, 12(1), 1–15.

Baker, A. (2014, February 17). Common Curriculum now has critics on the left. *New York Times*, A1, A13.

Bishop, J. P. (2012). "She's always been the smart one. I've always been the dumb one": Identities in the mathematics classroom. *Journal for Research in Mathematics Education,* 43(1), 34–74.

Calkins, L., Ehrenworth, M., and Lehman, C. (2012). *Pathways to the Common Core: Accelerating achievement.* Portsmouth, NH: Heinemann.

Carey-Webb, A. (1993). Racism and *Huckleberry Finn:* Censorship, dialogue, and change. *English Journal,* 82(7), 22–34.

Carey-Webb, A. (2001). Racism and *Huckleberry Finn:* Censorship, dialogue, and change. In *Literature and lives: A response-based, cultural studies approach to teaching English.* Urbana, IL: NCTE Press.

Cargo, M., Grams, G. D., Ottoson, J. M., Ward, P., and Green, L. W. (2003). Empowerment as fostering positive youth development and citizenship. *Journal of Health Behavior,* 27, 566–81.

Cassidy, J., Ziv, Y., Mehta, T. G., and Feeney, B. C. (2003). Feedback seeking in children and adolescents: Associations with self-perceptions, attachment representations, and depression. *Child Development,* 74(2), 612–28.

Clark, M. (1991). Social identity, peer relations, and academic competence of African American adolescents. *Education and Urban Society,* 24(1), 45–52.

Coleman, D., and Pimentel, S. (2012). *Revised publishers' criteria for the Common Core State Standards in English Language Arts and Literacy, grades 3–12.* Retrieved from http://www.corestandards.org/assets/Publishers_Criteria_for_3-12.pdf.

Common Core State Standards Initiative (n.d.). Common Core Standards criteria. Retrieved from http://www.edweek.org/media/standardscriteriavfinal.pdf.

Common Core State Standards Initiative (2013). Common Core Standards. Retrieved from http://www.corestandards.org.

Conchas, Gilberto Q. (2006). Uprooting children: Mobility, social capital and Mexican American underachievement. *Journal of Latinos and Education,* 5(2), 159–61.

Deal, N. (2013). Executive order issued May 15, 2013. Retrieved from https://gov.georgia.gov/press-releases/2013-05-15/deal-executive-order-protects-students-local-control.

Delpit, L. (1992). Acquisition of literate discourse: Bowing before the master? *Theory into Practice,* 31(4), 296–302.

Downey, M. (2014, February 4). Is it too late to stop Common Core in Georgia? *myAJC.com.* Retrieved from http://www.myajc.com/weblogs/get-schooled/2014/feb/04/too-late-stop-common-core-georgia/.

Fletcher, J. M., Lyons, G. R., Fuchs, L. S., and Barnes, M. A. (2007). *Learning disabilities: From identification to intervention.* New York: Springer.

Gee, J. P. (2000–2001). Identity as an analytic lens for research in education. *Review of Research in Education,* 25, 99–125.

Gee, J. P. (2003). *What video games have to teach us about learning and literacy.* New York: Palgrave Macmillan.

Gingrey, J. P. (2014). *We can save America.* Retrieved from gingrey.com.

Ginwright, S., and James, T. (2002). From assets to agents of change: Social justice, organizing, and youth development. *New Directions for Youth Development,* 96, 27–47.

Green, E. J., McCollum, V. C., and Hays, D. (2008). Teaching advocacy counseling within a social justice framework: Implications for school counselors and educators. *Journal for Social Action in Counseling and Psychology,* 1(2), 14–30.

Hatt, B. (2007). Street smarts vs. book smarts: The figured world of smartness in the lives of marginalized, urban youth. *Urban Review,* 39(2), 145–68.

Heibert, E. H., and Mesmer, H. A. E. (2013). Upping the ante of text complexity in the Common Core State Standards: Examining its potential impact on young readers. *Educational Researcher,* 42(1), 44–51.

Henry, A. (1992). African Canadian women teachers' activism: Recreating communities of caring and resistance. *Journal of Negro Education,* 61(3), 392–404.

Heron-Hruby, A., Hagood, M. C., and Alvermann, D. E. (2008). Switching places and looking to adolescents for the practices that shape school literacies. *Reading and Writing Quarterly: Overcoming Learning Difficulties,* 24(3), 311–34.

Huck Finn in context: A teaching guide. Adapted from a curriculum developed by the Cherry Hill, New Jersey, School District. Retrieved from http://www.pbs.org/wgbh/cultureshock/teachers/huck/index.html.

Jones, L. C., and Holland, A. (2013). Who blogs? Understanding the correlation of personality and blogging in cross-cultural discussions. *CALICO Journal*, 30, 92–117.

Just, O. (2010). Mark Twain, as a reporter, found recognition after story about Stamford brothers at sea. *Connecticut Post*, April 20. Retrieved from http://www.ctpost.com/news/article/Mark-Twain-as-a-reporter-found-recognition-456106.php.

Kahne, J., and Bailey, K. (1999). The role of social capital in youth development: The case of "I Have a Dream" programs. *Educational Evaluation and Policy Analysis*, 21(3), 321–43.

Kamil, M. L., Borman, G. D., Dole, J., Krai, C. C., Salinger, T., and Torgesen, J. (2008). *Improving adolescent literacy: Effective classroom and intervention practices; A practice guide.* Institute of Education Sciences, U.S. Department of Education, NCEE 2008-4027. Retrieved from: http://ies.ed.gov/ncee/wwc.

Knobel, M., and Lankshear, C. (Eds.). (2007). *A new literacies sampler.* New York: Peter Lang.

Lopez, M. L. and Stack, C. B. (2001). Social capital and the culture of power: Lessons from the field. In S. Saegert, J. P. Thompson, and M. R. Warren (Eds.), *Social capital and poor communities.* (pp. 57–76). The Russell Sage Foundation.

Malin, M. (1990). Why is life so hard for Aboriginal students in urban classrooms? *Aboriginal Child at School*, 18(1), 9–29.

Markus, H., and Nurius, P. (1986). Possible selves. *American Psychologist, 41*, 954–969.

McCallumore, K. M., and Sparapani, E. F. (2010). The importance of the ninth grade on high school graduation rates and student success in high school. *Education*, 130(3). 447–456.

McQuillan, P. J. (2005). Possibilities and pitfalls: A comparative analysis of student empowerment. *American Educational Research Journal*, 42(4), 639–670.

MetaMetrics. (n.d.). Lexile analyzer: Get a Lexile text measure. Retrieved from www.lexile.com/analyzer/.

MetaMetrics. (2013). Lexile map. Retrieved from http://cdn.lexile.com/m/cms_page_media/135/Lexile%20Map_8.5x11_FINAL_Updated_May_2013%20%284%29.pdf.

Mostafa, M. (2014). From freedom of expression to expression of freedom: Responding to socio-political change in the classroom. *Journal for Education in the Built Environment*, 9(1), 35–47.

Nation's Report Card (2013). 2013 Mathematics and Reading. Retrieved from http://nationsreportcard.gov/reading_math_2013/#/.

Neild, R. C., Stoner-Eby, S., and Fursten, F. (2008). Connecting entrance and departure: The transition to ninth grade and high school dropout. *Education and Urban Society*, 40(5), 543–69.

Noguera, P. A. (2001). Racial politics and the elusive quest for excellence and equity in education. *Education and Urban Society*, 34, 18–41.

Noguera, P. A., and Wing, J. Y. (2006). *Unfinished business: Closing the racial achievement gap in our schools.* San Francisco: Jossey-Bass.

O'Brien, D., Beach, R., and Scharber, C. (2007). "Struggling" middle schoolers: Engagement and literate competence in a reading writing intervention class. *Reading Psychology*, 28(1), 51–73.

Ogbu, J. U. (1987). Variability in minority school performance. *Anthropology of Education Quarterly*, 18, 312–34.

Ogbu, J. U. (1992). Adaptation to minority status and impact on school success. *Theory into Practice*, 31(4), 287–95.

Osborne, A. B. (1996). Practice into theory into practice: Culturally relevant practice for students we have marginalized and normalized. *Anthropology and Education Quarterly*, 27(3), 285–314.

Pearson, P. D. (2013). Research and the Common Core: Is the relationship viable? Keynote presented at the annual meeting of the American Reading Forum, Sanibel Island, Florida.

Perkins, M. (2009). Straight talk on race: Challenging the stereotypes in kids' books. *School Library Journal*. Retrieved from http://www.slj.com/2009/04/standards/straight-talk-on-race-challenging-the-stereotypes-in-kids-books/#_.

Plucker, J. A. (1998). The relationship between school climate conditions and student aspirations. *Journal of Educational Research*, 91(4), 240–46.

Ream, R. K., and Palardy, G. J. (2008). Reexamining social class differences in the availability and the educational utility of parental social capital. *American Educational Research Journal*, 45(2), 238–73.

Roche, J. (1999). Children: Rights, participation, and citizenship. *Childhood*, 6, 475–93.

Rosenblatt, L. (1978). *The reader, the text, the poem: The transactional theory of the literary work*. Carbondale: Southern Illinois Press.

Watts, R. J., and Flanagan, C. (2007). Pushing the envelope on youth civic engagement: A developmental and liberation psychology perspective. *Journal of Community Psychology*, 35(6), 779–92.

Winfrey, O. (2009). Jay-Z on the N-word. Video. Retrieved from http://www.oprah.com/oprah-show/jay-z-on-the-n-word-video.

Chapter Five

Strategies for Supporting Emergent Bilingual Students

Sanjuana Rodriguez

Introduction Classroom Example: Mrs. Rodriguez

Mrs. Rodriguez sits at a table ready to teach guided reading. She is in an elementary classroom serving as the ELL teacher. It's time for reading workshop, and all of the students are busy transitioning into their favorite time. The chatter of students reading and discussing what books they will pick to read is heard throughout the classroom. Suddenly, the classroom teacher enters the room and hears some of the students speaking Spanish. She scolds them for speaking their home language, "English only please. You can talk in Spanish at home, but at school we always need to speak in English." The two students look blankly at her and continue their work. The talking in Spanish stops and they proceed to speak only in English. The teacher, who is supposed to support the students' language learning, clearly sends the message that their home language is neither relevant nor welcome at school.

My interest in bilingualism in education stems from my own experiences of learning to speak English in the third grade after my family moved to the United States. As is the case for other emergent bilinguals in the United States, I entered an English-only environment that failed to see emerging bilingualism as an asset. For the first year of schooling in the United States, for half of each school day I was bused to a school that had been closed down. The only classrooms open there were for students learning English and students with behavior disorders. I spent half of the academic day with other students from across the district that—like me—were learning English.

The focus of this class was not only academics but also acculturation. For the rest of each school day, I was pulled out of the classroom for additional instruction in reading and math. As I reflected on my experiences as an

61

emergent bilingual, I realized how much the educational policies made me feel like an outsider. At a time when I wanted to fit in and settle into a new home, language, and culture, I was being isolated in the name of "good" practices that were designed, in theory, to help me.

THE EDUCATION OF EMERGENT BILINGUALS

It is projected that by the year 2050, Latinx will account for about 29 percent of the population in the United States compared to 14 percent in 2005 (Brown, 2014), and the number of Latinx children enrolled in U.S. schools will also increase. The Pew Hispanic Resource Center, in a study of the U.S. Census data, concluded that Latinx currently make up nearly one fourth of the students in U.S. schools (Fry and Lopez, 2012).

Despite the growth of Latinx students in U.S. schools, school curricula continue to exclude students who are culturally and linguistically diverse, including Latinx students. Latinx researchers and scholars have documented and called for instruction that uses emergent bilinguals students' social, cultural, and community resources (Garcia, 2005; Jimenez, 2003; González et al., 2005; Sánchez and Machado-Casas, 2009).

The demographics of teachers in the United States do not reflect the growing diversity in schools. Results from a study published by the U.S. Department of Education (2016) indicate that despite the growing diversity in students, the teaching force remain homogenous. In the 2011–2012 school year, white teachers account for 82 percent of total teachers in public schools while white students accounted for 51 percent of the total population.

The diversity in the teacher workforce has gradually increased over time. For example, in the 1987–1988 school year, white teachers accounted for 87 percent of public school teachers compared to 82 percent in the 2011–2012 school year. During that same time span, the number of Latinx teachers as increased from 3 percent to 8 percent of public school teachers. The U.S. Department of Education report establishes that "teachers of color are also overwhelmingly employed in public schools serving populations with relatively high proportions of students of color and public schools in urban communities" (2016, p. 7).

It is important for teachers to understand the varied literacy trajectories that emergent bilinguals can take as they learn additional languages. The conceptions teachers have of these students can impact the way that they interact with and teach this group of students. (Reeves, 2006; Walker, Shafer, and Liams, 2004; Yoon, 2008). Among the concerns that teachers have about working with emergent bilingual students is limited time and resources to work effectively (Gándara, Maxwell-Jolly, and Driscoll, 2005; Reeves, 2006).

Another factor that influences instruction for emergent bilinguals is the belief that "good teaching" is effective for all students, including students learning an additional language (Harper, de Jong, and Platt, 2008). Also important to consider is that teachers continue to be underprepared for teaching emergent bilingual students (De Jong and Harper, 2005; Gándara and Santibañez, 2016). Given the importance of students' language development for classroom success, all classroom teachers with emergent bilingual students need to understand the best practices for meeting the needs of students learning a new language. Gándara and Santibañez (2016) identify the qualities of effective teachers of emergent bilingual students; these include knowledge of language uses, forms, and mechanics; a feeling of efficacy in helping students achieve high standards; skills to build strong relationships; cultural knowledge and the skills to use that knowledge to inform the curriculum; and specific pedagogical skills.

Under No Child Left Behind (NCLB) (2001), the standard has been for students, including English Language Learners (ELLs), to be reading on grade level by third grade. Despite this increase in accountability for all students, the reading test scores for English Language Learners has not improved. NCLB brought attention to this gap because, for the first time, schools were required to report the standardized test scores for ELLs and how these scores compared to native English speakers.

WHAT'S IN A NAME? ENGLISH LANGUAGE LEARNERS VERSUS EMERGENT BILINGUALS

The term "English Language Learner" promotes a deficit view of students. The U.S. Department of Education has used two terms: "English Language Learners" (ELL) and "Limited English Proficiency (LEP)." These terms privilege the English language and ignore the potential of using the students' home language as a resource for learning. For this reason, I have chosen to adopt the term "emergent bilingual" (Reyes, 2006; Garcia, Kleifgen and Falchi, 2008).

This term is has been used by scholars of bilingual education to emphasize the potential that students have in becoming bilingual or multilingual. It also validates individual students by recognizing that they already speak one or more languages. Because much of the academic literature still refers to emergent bilingual students as English Language Learners, I will often use the terms when citing those specific documents.

HISTORICAL CONTEXT IN THE EDUCATION OF EMERGENT BILINGUALS

The historical context of bilingual education in the United States is important for understanding the current context for educating emergent bilinguals. Historically, the courts have played an important part in dictating language education policy for students learning an additional language.

Recent increases in immigration in the United States have made finding the best way to educate bilingual students urgent. There has been a long history of controversy regarding the best instructional methods for teaching students who are learning English: "The use of non-English languages for instructional purposes in the U.S. has been controversial since the early 18th century, with alternating cycles of acceptance and rejection depending on the relationship of the U.S. with the countries from which immigrants came" (Gándara et al., 2010, p. 22).

In 1968 the federal government enacted the Bilingual Education Act in an effort to "aid and monitor the education of English Language Learners" (Ovando, 2003, p. 8). The act provided funds to programs that supported language learning, but it did not take a position on the methods of English instruction.

In 1974, a group of Chinese parents in San Francisco brought forth a discrimination suit because their children did not understand what the teachers were saying. The Supreme Court ruled in *Lau v. Nichols* that the San Francisco school board was violating Chinese-speaking students' rights to equal education under the Civil Rights Act of 1964 (Losen and Skiba, 2010). The San Francisco school system had to provide the students with "access to the same curriculum as their English speaking peers" by providing supplemental English instruction (Losen and Skiba, 2010, p. 196). The court ruled that "districts must take affirmative steps to rectify the language deficiency in order to open its instructional program to these students" (*Lau v. Nichols*, 1974).

The Equal Educational Opportunity Act (EEOA) passed by Congress after the *Lau* decision extended the order to all schools. The *Lau* decision made states responsible for providing equal opportunities to students learning English. However, it did not specify the method for providing English instruction, and "it did not prescribe specific curricular content or methodology to restore the civil rights of the students in question" (Losen and Skiba, 2010, p. 9).

Since the 1980s, the controversy has shifted to the call to provide instruction through English-only programs. The rhetoric in the last thirty years has supported "sink or swim" methods in which students are placed in classrooms and expected to learn English with no additional support. For example, California's Proposition 227, which passed in 1998, required that instruction would be in English (Ovando, 2003, p. 13). Additionally, thirty states have enacted legislation or constitutional amendments that make English the "official" language of the state (Crawford, 2004).

The English-only movement continues to rise with "increasing immigration, rising numbers of ELs and a 'close the borders' mentality gripping the nation" (Gándara et al., 2010, p. 26). In fact, all references to bilingual education were removed in the reauthorization of the Elementary and Secondary Education Act (ESEA), which became the No Child Left Behind Act of 2002. The Office of Bilingual Education was also renamed the office of English Language Acquisition, Language Enhancement, and Academic Achievement for Limited English Proficient Students (Gándara et al., 2010, p. 26).

Currently, classroom instruction for emergent bilingual students varies from state to state and depends on the number of emergent bilingual students in schools. Teachers' practices can be shaped by the policies that mandate the language of instruction, and these policies are informed by ideologies that in turn impact teachers and classrooms.

As stated earlier, the adoption of NCLB in 2001 created a need for standardized curricula to be solely in English because of the growing demands for emergent bilinguals to perform at the same levels as native English speakers. Spring notes, "State standardized curricula negated efforts for school curricula to reflect students' home cultures by requiring all students to study the same standardized curriculum" (U.S. Department of Education, 2016, p. 142). This policy led to the triumph of English-only education for students in the United States. Currently, very few states allow for the use of students' language in the official school curriculum.

THE CASE FOR CULTURALLY RESPONSIVE PEDAGOGY

Culturally responsive pedagogy recognizes the importance of students' cultural experience (Ladson-Billings, 1994). It not only acknowledges students' rich cultural experience but also celebrates those experiences and uses them for instruction. Fundamental to this pedagogy is the idea that all students should have equitable access to education.

Hayes and Juarez make the case for culturally responsive pedagogy. They state that "there is no culturally responsive pedagogy and social justice spoken in many public schools and teacher preparation programs" (2012, p. 2) but that this should be happening, considering the growing number of students who are culturally and linguistically diverse. With this in mind, the following section describes some of the characteristics of culturally responsive pedagogy and how teachers may implement some of these in their own practice.

POSITIVE PERSPECTIVES ON PARENTS AND FAMILIES

The first characteristic of culturally responsive pedagogy is having and build-ing positive relationships with the students' parents and families. This is important because children's first teachers are their parents, and teachers should view the parents as partners. Teachers should be able to see parents and families from an asset-based perspective despite differences in culture or values. This may mean that teachers have to redefine what they consider parental involvement.

As a classroom teacher, I often heard others complaining at the lack of parent involvement at the Title I school where I taught. On occasion, I also engaged in these discussions and wished that I could have had parents help-ing me in the classroom. As I learned more about the families and the home lives of many of my students, I began to understand that parental involve-ment might look different. Many of the parents had more than one job and still came home and ensured that their child was ready for school the next day. I learned that the parents that I worked with had very high expectations about their children's success in school.

Much of the research around funds of knowledge has been focused on helping teachers create positive perspectives and relationships with families (González et al., 2005). González and colleagues researched teachers that worked primarily with Latinx families. Their work helped teachers to be-come ethnographers—to go into the homes of their students to learn from them. The teachers used what they learned from the home visits and infused this knowledge about students' cultural assets into the curriculum. This work emphasizes that all students have funds of knowledge in their homes that can be tapped as a resource and used in the classroom.

This is a departure from traditional situations such as parent-teacher con-ferences where the teacher teaches or informs the parents. Instead, teachers went into the students' homes to conduct interviews and observations. The teachers then reflected on this learning and collaborated with others to design curriculum based on the funds of knowledge found in the home.

Similarly, Ladson-Billings's work (2001) underscores that teachers must understand students' lives and cultures. Teachers must have an understand-ing of the role that culture plays in education. Ladson-Billings (2001) also points out that knowing about students' cultures is not enough. Teachers must use students' culture as a basis for learning.

HIGH EXPECTATIONS

Another characteristic of CRP is having and communicating high expecta-tions for students who are culturally and linguistically diverse. This characteristic fits within the ethic of care framework, which contends that student success is due to teachers who have high expectations of students (Antrop-González and De Jesús, 2006).

Several studies have focused on how caring relationships—or having an ethic of care— can help Latinx students be academically successful (Antrop-González and De Jesús, 2006; Rolón-Dow, 2005; Valenzuela, 2009). Part of establishing a caring community is creating an environment that supports and encourages caring attitudes.

In their study of two high schools located in predominantly Latinx communities, Antrop-González and De Jesús (2006) investigated how teachers practiced "critical care." Their study demonstrated the importance of high expectation for students who are culturally and linguistically diverse. The researchers concluded that such high expectations helped students know that they were cared for. Thus, critical care in classrooms involves both building relationships with students and providing an environment that expects students to do well academically. Antrop-González and De Jesús (2006) contend that when working with culturally and linguistically diverse students, teachers should seek opportunities to help students reach their full potential instead of lowering expectations for them.

CRITICAL CONSCIOUSNESS

Teachers using CRP have to be "more self-conscious, critical, and analytical of one's own teaching beliefs and behaviors" (Gay and Kirkland, 2003). Critical consciousness is a construct of *conscientizaçáo*, a concept attributed to Paulo Freire for interpreting and critiquing one's own experiences. It is a process of "learning how to read in relation to the awakening of . . . consciousness" (1974, p. 38) and allows one the possibility to not only "be in the world, but to engage in relations with the world" (p. 39). This idea allows teachers to see and reflect on their own privilege. Developing a critical consciousness also gives teachers the opportunity to see the barriers to equity in education that children who are culturally and linguistically diverse experience.

PRACTICAL STRATEGIES FOR SUPPORTING EMERGENT BILINGUAL STUDENTS IN READING

Emergent bilingual students can be supported by providing rich literacy opportunities that validate their own experiences. For instance, teachers can provide access to multicultural literature. All students, including emergent bilingual students, need opportunities to see themselves and others in texts. Rudine Bishop refers to this as "windows" and "mirrors":

> Books are sometimes windows, offering views of worlds that may be real or
> imagined, familiar or strange. These windows are also sliding glass doors, and
> readers have only to walk through in imagination to become part of whatever
> world has been created and recreated by the author. When lighting conditions
> are just right, however, a window can also be a mirror. Literature transforms
> human experience and reflects it back to us, and in that reflection we can see
> our own lives and experiences as part of the larger human experience. Read-
> ing, then, becomes a means of self-affirmation, and readers often seek their
> mirrors in books. (1990, p. ix)

However, there are still a limited number of books that represent the experience of Latinx students in the United States (Braden and Rodriguez, 2016).
The Cooperative Children's Book Center (CCBC) documents the number of
books that are published and received each year and provides statistics based
on books published by and about African Americans, Latinx, people from the
Asian Pacific, and American Indians.

For 2015, the CCBC received a total number of 3,400 books. Of these,
269 were about African Americans, 42 were about American Indians, 113
were about Asian Pacific or Asian Pacific Americans, and 82 were about
Latinx (Cooperative Children's Book Center, 2016). Reading texts that allow
for children to see themselves and also to learn about the experience of others
is important. Teachers must also keep in mind that having books that feature
diverse characters is not enough. Discussions around others' experiences will
help students to see the complexities of culture.

Read-alouds are another strategy for reading instruction for emergent
bilingual students. Read-alouds are a tool for both older and younger readers.
Research indicates that read-alouds can build reading skills (Giroir et al.,
2015) Including daily read-alouds can also improve students' comprehension
and vocabulary development (McKeown and Beck, 2004). Interactive read-
alouds also provide a meaningful way for students to engage in conversations
about reading with other students.

Another suggestion for teachers is to include many opportunities for
emerging bilingual students to develop sophisticated vocabularies. Vocabulary instruction is very important, particularly for emergent bilingual students, because if student do not know the meaning of a word, then they will
have difficulty understanding the content. In fact, vocabulary knowledge has
been found to be the best predictor of success for emergent bilingual students
(White, Graves, and Slater, 1990).

Vocabulary instruction must be explicit. Teachers cannot assume that
emergent bilinguals' academic vocabulary will improve by simple exposure
to words. Vaughn and colleagues have developed effective interventions in
learning vocabulary for emergent bilingual students (Vaughn et al., 2005;
Vaughn et al., 2006). Those include explicit instruction in oral language,
listening comprehension, and reading comprehension; read-alouds with ex-

plicit vocabulary instruction; word study and phonics strategy study; and repeated readings. In addition to vocabulary instruction being explicit, it is also important for vocabulary to be learned in context (Beck, McKeown, and Kucan, 2013).

STRATEGIES FOR SUPPORTING EMERGENT BILINGUAL STUDENTS IN WRITING

Just as emergent students need to be supported in reading, they should be equally supported in writing. One of the most important things that teachers can do is to allow students the opportunity to write every day. The writing process is something that has to be learned and practiced every day (Calkins and Ehrenworth, 2016). In order for students to practice writing, teachers have to provide protected time during the school day.

In their study of classroom writing practices, Gilbert and Graham (2010) found that in grades four through six, students spent an average of twenty-five minutes writing across the day. This is simply not enough time for students to develop as writers. Students need to see reading and writing as interrelated processes and understand that they are valued and supported in all literacy practices that take place in the classroom.

Teachers can begin the year with an oral storytelling component. In this strategy, students have an opportunity to talk about what is important to them and what they value. The stories that students tell become the basis for the first entries in their writing notebooks. Perry argues that "like print literacy, storytelling represents a purposeful sociocultural practice shaped by and closely linked to a community's beliefs, values, and attitudes" (2008, p. 321).

Oral storytelling at the beginning of the year and before launching writing workshops or units can create a sense of community. Additionally, having students tell their stories allows the students to see that who they are as individuals, their culture, and their language are important. It is also important for the teacher to tell his or her stories, as this allows students to view the teacher as a writer.

Emergent bilingual students can be supported in writing by allowing them to use their home language as a resource for writing (Laman, 2013). This concept would look different depending on the levels of English-language proficiency in the classroom. For instance, students could be allowed to write their stories in the first language first and then translate them into English, thus allowing them to produce bilingual texts.

Teachers can also use students' first language in the bilingual creation of anchor charts. Many teachers of young students create anchor charts that serve as supports for students when they are writing. These could include family words, places, and words related to games. These charts could be translated into multiple languages to support emergent bilingual students as they are writing.

It is important for teachers to invite students' lives into the classroom. Students have to know that their experiences are valued. Different strategies can help teachers do this. At the beginning of the year, students can create heart maps (Heard, 1999). Heart mapping is simply having students think about the things that are important in their lives. Students actually write specific phrases about important moments, important people in their lives, and experiences that they will never forget. Students create sections for each of these ideas and others. This becomes a basis for students to write stories, poems, and memoirs. Again, this strategy validates students' lives and allows their experiences to become part of the curriculum.

CONCLUSION

As the number of emergent bilingual students in the United States continues to grow, teachers have to be supported by policies and provided with resources to help them understand the literacy development of this group of students. Educating emergent bilingual students is more than just good teaching (De Jong and Harper, 2005; Gándara and Santibañez, 2016).

Educating emerging bilingual students means that teachers must get to know their students, families, and communities. Teachers must also provide explicit instruction while allowing students to use their home language as a support for learning. Students' lives must be viewed as assets and be interwoven into the curriculum. Teachers must become close observers of the literacy development of students and be ready to support them through inclusionary practices that affirm students' lives. Finally, teachers have to continue to work toward the closing of the opportunity gap by recognizing inequities in education for emergent bilinguals (Garcia, Kleifgen, and Falchi, 2008) and working toward authentic literacy experiences that support this group of students.

REFERENCES

Antrop-González, R., and De Jesús, A. (2006). Toward a theory of critical care in urban small school reform: Examining structures and pedagogies of caring in two Latino community-based schools. *International Journal of Qualitative Studies in Education*, 19(4), 409–33.

Beck, I. L., McKeown, M. G., and Kucan, L. (2013). *Bringing words to life: Robust vocabulary instruction*. New York: Guilford.

Bishop, R. S. (1990). Mirrors, windows, and sliding glass doors. *Perspectives*, 6(3), ix–xi.

Braden, E., and Rodriguez, S. (2016). Beyond mrrors and windows: A critical content analysis of Latino children's books. *Journal of Language and Literacy Education*, 12(2), 56–83.

Brown, A. (2014). The US Hispanic population has increased sixfold since 1970. Pew Research Center, *Fact Tank*, February 26. Retrieved from http://www.pewresearch.org/fact-tank/2014/02/26/the-u-s-hispanic-population-has-increased-sixfold-since-1970/.

Calkins, L., and Ehrenworth, M. (2016). Growing extraordinary writers: Leadership decisions to raise the level of writing across a school and a district. *Reading Teacher*, 70(1), 7–18.

Cooperative Children's Book Center. (2016). Publishing statistics on children's books about people of color and first/Native nations and by people of color and first/Native Nations Authors and Illustrators. School of Education, University of Wisconsin-Madison. Retrieved from http://ccbc.education.wisc.edu/books/pcstats.asp.

Crawford, J. (2004). *Educating English learners: Language diversity in the classroom*. Bilingual Education Services.

De Jong, E. J., and Harper, C. A. (2005). Preparing mainstream teachers for English-language learners: Is being a good teacher good enough? *Teacher Education Quarterly*, 32(2), 101–24.

Freire, P. (1974). *Pedagogy of the oppressed* (trans. M. B. Ramos). New York: Seabury Press.

Fry, R., and Lopez, M. H. (2012). *Hispanic student enrollments reach new highs in 2011*. Washington, DC: Pew Hispanic Center. Retrieved from http://www.pewhispanic.org/2012/08/20/hispanic-student-enrollments-reach-new-highs-in-2011/.

Gándara, P., Losen, D., August, D., Uriarte, M., Gómez, M. C., and Hopkins, M. (2010). Forbidden language: A brief history of U.S. language policy. In P. Gándara and M. Hopkins (Eds.), *Forbidden language: English learners and restrictive language policies* (20–33). New York: Teachers College Press.

Gándara, P., Maxwell-Jolly, J., and Driscoll, A. (2005). *Listening to teachers of English Language Learners: A survey of California teachers' challenges, experiences, and professional development needs*. Policy Analysis for California Education. Santa Cruz, CA: Center for the Future of Teaching and Learning.

Gándara, P., and Santibañez, L. (2016). The teachers our English Language Learners need. *Educational Leadership*, 73(5), 32–37.

García, E. E. (2005). *Teaching and learning in two languages: Bilingualism and schooling in the United States*. New York: Teachers College Press.

García, O., Kleifgen, J. A., and Falchi, L. (2008). *From English Language Learners to Emergent Bilinguals*. Equity Matters, Research Review 1. New York: Campaign for Educational Equity, Teachers College, Columbia University.

Gay, G., and Kirkland, K. (2003). Developing cultural critical consciousness and self-reflection in preservice teacher education. *Theory into Practice*, 42(3), 181–87.

Gilbert, J., and Graham, S. (2010). Teaching writing to elementary students in grades 4–6: A national survey. *Elementary School Journal*, 110(4), 494–518.

Giroir, S., Grimaldo, L. R., Vaughn, S., and Roberts, G. (2015). Interactive read-alouds for English learners in the elementary grades. *Reading Teacher*, 68(8), 639–48.

González, N., Moll, L., and Amanti, C. (2005). *Funds of knowledge: Theorizing practices in households, communities, and classrooms*. New York: Routledge.

Harper, C. A., de Jong, E. J., and Platt, E. J. (2008). Marginalizing English as a second language teacher expertise: The exclusionary consequence of No Child Left Behind. *Language Policy*, 7(3), 267–84.

Hayes, C., and Juarez, B. (2012). There is no culturally responsive teaching spoken here: A critical race perspective. *Democracy and Education*, 20(1), 1.

Heard, G. (1999). *Awakening the heart: Exploring poetry in elementary and middle school*. Portsmouth, NH: Heinemann.

Jiménez, R. T. (2003). Literacy and Latino students in the United States: Some considerations, questions, and new directions. *Reading Research Quarterly*, 38(1), 122–28.

Ladson-Billings, G. (1994). *The dreamkeepers*. San Francisco: Jossey-Bass.

Ladson-Billings, G. (2001). *Crossing over to Canaan: The journey of new teachers in diverse classrooms*. San Francisco: Jossey-Bass.

Laman, T. T. (2013). *From ideas to words: Writing strategies for English Language Learners*. Portsmouth, NH: Heinemann.

Lau v. Nichols. (1974). 414, U.S. 563.

Losen, D. J., and Skiba, R. J. (2010). Suspended education: Urban middle schools in crisis. *The Civil Rights Project*. Retrieved from https://escholarship.org/uc/item/8fh0s5dv.

McKeown, M. G., and Beck, I. L. (2004). Transforming knowledge into professional development resources: Six teachers implement a model of teaching for understanding text. *Elementary School Journal*, 105(5), 391–408.

No Child Left Behind (NCLB). (2001). PL 107-110. Washington, DC: U.S. Department of Education.

Olsen, L. (2010). *Reparable harm: Fulfilling the unkept promise of educational opportunity for California's long term English learners*. Long Beach, CA: Californians Together.

Ovando, C. J. (2003). Bilingual education in the United States: Historical development and current issues. *Bilingual Research Journal*, 27(1), 1–24.

Perry, K. H. (2008). From storytelling to writing: Transforming literacy practices among Sudanese refugees. *Journal of Literacy Research*, 40(3), 317–58.

Reeves, J. R. (2006). Secondary teacher attitudes toward including English-language learners in mainstream classrooms. *Journal of Educational Research*, 99(3), 131–43.

Reyes, I. (2006). Exploring connections between emergent biliteracy and bilingualism. *Journal of Early Childhood Literacy*, 6(3), 267–92.

Rodriguez, S., and Braden, E. (2016). Beyond mirrors and windows: A critical content analysis of Latino children's books. *Journal of Literacy and Language Education*, 12(2), 56–83.

Rolón-Dow, R. (2005). Critical care: A color (full) analysis of care narratives in the schooling experiences of Puerto Rican girls. *American Educational Research Journal*, 42(1), 77–111.

Sánchez, P., and Machado-Casas, M. (2009). At the intersection of transnationalism, Latina/o immigrants, and education. *The High School Journal*, 92(4), 3–15.

Spring, J. (2016). *Deculturalization and the struggle for equality: A brief history of the education of dominated cultures in the United States*. New York: Routledge.

U.S. Department of Education. (2016). *The state of racial diversity in the educator workforce*. Washington, DC: Policy and Program Studies Service, Office of Planning, Evaluation, and Policy Development, U.S. Department of Education. Retrieved from http://www2.ed.gov/rschstat/eval/highered/racial-diversity/state-racial-diversity-workforce.pdf.

Valenzuela, A. (2009). *Subtractive schooling: US-Mexican youth and the politics of caring*. New York: State University of New York Press.

Vaughn, S., Mathes, P., Linan-Thompson, S., Cirino, P., Carlson, C., Pollard-Durodola, S., Elsa Cardenas-Hagan, E., and Francis, D. (2006). Effectiveness of an English intervention for first-grade English language learners at risk for reading problems. *Elementary School Journal*, 107, 153–81.

Vaughn, S., Mathes, P., Linan-Thompson, S., and Francis, D. J. (2005). Teaching English language learners at risk for reading disabilities to read: Putting research into practice. *Learning Disabilities Research and Practice*, 20, 58–67.

Walker, A., Shafer, J., and Liams, M. (2004). "Not in my classroom": Teacher attitudes towards English language learners in the mainstream classroom. *NABE Journal of Research and Practice*, 2(1), 130–60.

White, T. G., Graves, M. F., and Slater, W. H. (1990). Growth of reading vocabulary in diverse elementary schools: Decoding and word meaning. *Journal of Educational Psychology*, 82(2), 281–90.

Yoon, B. (2008). Uninvited guests: The influence of teachers' roles and pedagogies on the positioning of English language learners in the regular classroom. *American Educational Research Journal*, 45(2), 495–522.

Chapter Six

Culturally Relevant Teaching

The Impact of Beliefs on Practices

Natasha Thornton

Introduction Classroom Example: Cori

"It's just the whole idea of code-switching and our children being able to do that. And we come in and speak Standard English and we see our children and they are not speaking it then we, well I, get upset because that's not how you are supposed to speak and they don't know the difference. And I don't how to . . . I don't know what to do . . . and I know that it's a black cultural thing where we don't know. Well, in any language there is a way you speak at home or how you speak when you are comfortable, and it should not be how you speak in a professional setting" (Cori, second day of professional development).

Teacher education programs are unwavering when it comes to the importance of reflection. Examining experiences to develop deeper understandings and to make informed decisions for future instruction is essential. More specifically, examining beliefs that relate to race, language, and culture is critical for teachers to provide a just education for all students. The opening vignette reflects the kinds of beliefs that teachers must wrestle with in order to implement inclusive instruction.

A variety of languages and cultures are represented in society, yet many are not valued. Teachers, as human beings in society, also have beliefs and philosophies that favor certain experiences, languages, and norms.

Volumes of research have addressed the cognitive, emotional, and psychological damage that can occur when students' lives are not validated during the learning process, yet this significant educational concern has yet to be considered in educational reforms. Teachers are the most significant factor when it comes to student learning (Allington, 2002); hence, if a teacher's beliefs negatively affect student learning, interrogating personal beliefs is the first and most critical step.

Five teachers, all African American women, volunteered to join the professional development at their Title I elementary school, which had a predominately African American population. The doctoral student conducting the study facilitated the professional development and was a former teacher at the school. Although the students in this school reflected many of the racial and cultural norms of their students, they knew that it was necessary to gain more understanding about how their beliefs and perceptions could affect their students.

This study was conducted as a formative experiment with the goal of shifting teachers' beliefs and practices to be more inclusive of the values and norms of the culturally and linguistically diverse students. This chapter depicts some of the shifts that occurred in teachers' beliefs and practices as they participated in ongoing, critical, professional learning centered on culturally relevant literacy instruction.

I will discuss the importance of examining beliefs when there is a cultural mismatch between teachers and students. Cultural relevance will be described as a framework to value students' lives and build on their cultural and linguistic resources during instruction.

TEACHERS' BELIEFS

Along with four other elementary school teachers, Cori took part in professional learning that focused on culturally relevant literacy instruction. These teachers were interested in learning how they could better support students at the predominately African American school where they taught. During this discussion, the teachers contemplated the notion that African American Vernacular English (AAVE), or Ebonics, should be valued just as much as Standard English (SE).

Cori, a third-grade teacher, was very open about some of the tensions that she had with the language her students used at school. She recognized that everyone speaks a relaxed language in informal settings but believed Standard English should be spoken at school and in professional settings. This belief was common among most of the teachers, as it is a widely held belief in our society.

Speakers of various dialects and English vernaculars, such as those using Ebonics or having a Southern accent, are often viewed as lacking in intelligence. This set of beliefs about language in the classroom is of grave importance, as U.S. classrooms are extremely diverse. Teachers need to have spaces where they can consider the impact that culture and language have on the instructional process and evaluate their beliefs in order to provide a more inclusive education for all students.

THE IMPORTANCE OF EXAMINING BELIEFS

Although volumes of educational research have been written about how to develop successful students, Lazar et al. (2012) declare there is an intellectual genocide of many students who are racially and culturally diverse. These scholars ask the important question, "How is it possible that America's public schools are failing so many students?" (p. 2). The status quo privileges white English speakers, therefore enabling one group to have an advantage over others in school and in society (Kincheloe and McLaren, 2002).

Many curricula and educational structures value dominant cultural norms, and many students of color and low-income students are marginalized during the learning process (Kesler, 2011). Paris (2012) insists that America's goal of access and equity in education is a goal that the working class and people of color learn to write and speak more like the white middle class. Schooling structures in America have been shaped by this belief.

A person's identity is intimately tied to their first language (Delpit, 2006; Smitherman, 2006), and the goal of teachers should be to value the language use of their students. Many African American students speak a variation of Standard English, such as African American Vernacular English, which often situates them as deficient or inferior. Language disparities between students and teachers have been a large factor in the underachievement and labeling of students. For instance, black students in Ann Arbor, Michigan, were placed in remediation and special education classes by teachers who felt they had a language deficiency because they spoke AAVE (Perry, 1997). Black students from Martin Luther King Jr. Elementary School sued the Ann Arbor school for not recognizing the social, cultural, and economic factors that impact learning. Sixty-six percent of the plaintiff children were classified as special needs in the predominately white school district in an affluent town. The negative perceptions that the teachers had of AAVE (Perry, 1997) resulted in students being excluded and silenced. Many African American scholars of language and education suggest that the cause of educational problems for African American children is not their language but the educational system's response to the language (Delpit, 2006).

Au (1998) emphasizes that students' poor academic achievement generally is not due to limited English proficiency. Rather, it is due to the exclusion or limited use of instruction in the home language or to the low status given the home language in schooling. Therefore, in comparison to white middle-class students who speak Standard English, students with linguistic differences have limited opportunity to use existing language skills as the foundation for learning to read and write.

Gupta (2010) conducted a study in which she examined teachers' perceptions about the impact of dialect on the educational achievement of students who speak AAVE in the United States and found that the majority of the teachers in the study saw AAVE as a deficit to learning. Based on self reports, 63 percent of the teachers disagreed with the statement that AAVE was an adequate language system, 54 percent agreed that students who speak AAVE will have communication problems in the classroom, and 58 percent believed that students who speak AAVE will have problems reading. Additionally, 73 percent believed that they would have problems in writing.

Gupta concludes that educators need a good understanding and knowledge of language variability in order to make educational decisions that ensure effective instruction. Green (2002) suggests that educators be knowledgeable about the rules of AAVE and understand that it is a systematic variety of Standard English. This would prevent a negative view of AAVE users and decrease the number of students labeled as learning disabled or at-risk because of the vernacular they use.

CULTURAL MISMATCH

The ethnic and racial makeup in U.S. public schools reflects a very diverse population. White students make up less than 50 percent of students, but the majority of the teachers are white, middle-class women (Kena et al., 2014). The cultural and linguistic differences between teachers and students can create a barrier to building on students' literacy experiences during instruction.

Culture reflects beliefs, values, norms, and perspectives and is influenced by race, ethnicity, socioeconomic level, educational level, religion, and the neighborhood and region of the country. When teachers' cultural beliefs align with the norms of mainstream education, valuing educational mandates, standardized curriculum, and high-stakes testing over the cultural and linguistic needs of students, cultural mismatches result.

When African American teachers have African American students, the cultural mismatch emerges from socioeconomic and educational differences between the teachers and the families that they serve (Wynter-Hoyte, 2014). Disrupting mainstream thinking is vital to disrupting inequities that reproduce oppression, such as the "pull yourself up by the boot straps" mentality and the notion that Standard English is superior to other variations of English.

When success in our society is measured using white, middle-class norms, the cultural and linguistic practices of all other communities of people are negated. Also, when diverse students are not represented in the texts and materials offered in school, they may wonder, "Where are the books and languages that reflect me?" (Nieto, 2009). That disconnect often causes them to disengage from school. Because of the mismatch between students' home cultures and the structure of mainstream education, teachers must make learning culturally relevant in order to promote academic achievement for students of color.

CULTURALLY RELEVANT APPROACH

Culturally relevant pedagogy (CRP) is a theoretical and pedagogical approach that addresses a major goal of multicultural education: to give students an equal chance to experience educational success and mobility (Banks, 2004). Multicultural education and CRP are frameworks that support the learning of all students (Au and Jordan, 1981; Mohatt and Erickson, 1982; Moll et al., 1992). CRP uses "students' culture in order to maintain it and to transcend the negative effects of the dominant culture" (Ladson-Billings, 1994, p. 17).

CRP provides teachers with ways of thinking about diverse students within an educational and societal context and offers tenets to operate within their beliefs to provide a relevant and equitable education to students. Villegas and Lucas (2007) urge that teaching students from diverse backgrounds and historically marginalized groups is more involved than applying specialized techniques; it demands a new approach to teaching that is rooted in an understanding of the role of culture and language in learning.

Therefore, in order for teachers to be culturally relevant, they have to believe that all cultures, not just their own culture or mainstream culture, are worth maintaining. Teachers need to identify and offset injustices, such as the misalignment of curriculum and instruction with what students actually need to learn.

Professional development should be rooted in teachers' experiences and beliefs, and teachers should reflect on their existing beliefs and behaviors so that they can become more receptive to alternative perspectives (Kuzborska, 2011; Richardson et al., 1991). Milner (2009) argues that it is critical for teachers of African American students to be well educated.

PROFESSIONAL LEARNING THAT IMPACTS BELIEFS AND PRACTICES

A number of research studies addressing the specific knowledge and attitudes relevant to teaching diverse students have taken place in school districts in urban areas and districts with large populations of culturally and linguistical-

ly diverse students. However, few studies have focused on professional development that centers on teachers' understanding of the culture and language development of students, the demands that mainstream education
places on culturally diverse students (Clair, 1993), and teachers' own beliefs
and implicit biases.

Few studies (Knight and Wiseman, 2005; Milner, 2009; Patton, 2011)
have examined culturally relevant professional development, and none has
focused explicitly on the impact of professional development on teachers'
practices around culturally relevant pedagogy. Likewise, in their review of
fifty-six articles on professional development for teachers of diverse students, Knight and Wiseman (2005) found that that little evidence exists for
determining the impact of professional development on teacher and student
outcomes.

In the study under consideration here, the professional learning was designed to provide teachers with research-based theories to help them consider
the historical and social factors that frame the educational issues facing people of color today. Readings and discussion protocols addressed culture,
language, curriculum, and educational policy. The study was conducted in
two parts.

The first part of the intervention was twenty hours of professional development (five hours per day for four days, which took place during the summer) focusing on culturally relevant pedagogy and literacy instruction (Ladson-Billings, 1994), and the second part included classroom observations and
debriefing meetings during the first semester of the school year, from Sep-
tember to January. At the conclusion of the four-day professional development program during the summer, two participants were selected as focal
teachers.

The researcher conducted classroom observations and supported the
teachers as they implemented culturally relevant literacy instruction in their
classrooms. This allowed the researcher to gain in-depth knowledge of what
the teachers learned and the beliefs they developed during the four-day professional development session, as well as how that knowledge and those
beliefs impacted their instructional practice.

The three other teachers—Carolyn, Cori, and Samantha—participated in
the debriefing sessions and served as continuous support for the focal group.
The researcher interviewed the teachers, took classroom observation data,
and audiorecorded the debriefing sessions to collect data documenting shifts.

Culturally relevant pedagogy is a not a set of strategies to be implemented
with students. Rather, it is a set of principles that guide teachers' beliefs and
instruction as they seek to meet the needs of their culturally diverse students.
Therefore, the teachers were not only taught strategies but were also engaged
in critical dialogue on research related to culture and language development,

and they were encouraged to develop their own understandings of CRP to guide their literacy instruction.

The teachers also engaged in critical self-reflection. They shared stories about students and parents about whom they had originally had negative perceptions that had changed once they interacted more closely with them. Being honest about these stories was critical for teachers since experiences are critical for examining beliefs. The teachers' varying perspectives pushed them to be more open and accepting.

SHIFTS IN BELIEFS AND PRACTICES

As a result of engaging in the professional development for this study, all of the teachers developed understandings about students' experiences and knowledge that can be used as catalysts for curriculum development and learning. All of the teachers saw their students' experiences and language in more positive ways.

Bridgette valued her individual kindergarten students' experiences, whereas Monica empathized with children's family lives and backgrounds, which led her to discuss sociopolitical issues with her fourth graders. Excerpts from the teachers' interviews and group debriefing sessions demonstrate how their beliefs began to influence their teaching. Though all of their practices were not inclusive, these shifts represent teachers' initial steps in framing their instruction with CRP.

Bridgette's Shifts in Beliefs and Practices

At the beginning of the study, Bridgette knew that valuing students and relying on their experiences were essential to learning, but she also struggled with that belief. In her first interview, Bridgette stated that there was "a different caliber of students" at Red Cove when the Magnet Program was there. She specified that most of her current students lived in single-parent homes, lived with their grandparents, or were in foster care.

She stated that most of the magnet students were on grade level at the beginning of the year, but that changed with a shift in student demographics. Despite indicating a desire to value students' cultures and home life, she appears to experience a conflict in her thinking around the resources these students bring to school. This may be because her experiences as a middle-class, African American educator and mother differed from the experiences of the students she was currently teaching.

Bridgette was cognizant about her beliefs and, during the four-day professional development session, she thought a lot about how to bridge her students' out-of-school experiences with classroom learning. She acknowledged that she still had some work to do around perceptions of students.

> Yes, I have shifted some. Hopefully, I'm more open to how students' back-
> grounds affect their performance in the classroom. I used to be more biased. I
> remember I used to judge single parents and kids by their hairstyles. I am
> aware of those biases now so I can separate how I feel about those kids from
> what they really are before I get to know them. (Post–professional develop-
> ment interview, July 30, 2013)

Bridgette's experiences in professional development helped her become
more aware of her biases. Once the school year began, she became more
intentional about connecting her students' lives with the state literacy and
writing standards. In turn, she reframed this knowledge in her writing curriculum plan to incorporate culturally relevant lessons that reflected students'
lives and connected to writing.

   During her daily read-aloud, she provided a longer discussion so that her
students had time to share their personal experiences in class. These discussions served as brainstorming for students' journal time. Bridgette's students
responded by writing in meaningful ways that connected personal knowledge
and the texts.

> When I see a standard, I think, what story can I choose, what I can read to
> make the students a part of this (as opposed just what related to their lives to
> make school more interesting, but a direct connection of CRP to standards)? I
> look at the standards to see what kind of text I can use to teach this and relate
> to the students. I intentionally look at standards where before I just read books
> that were relevant or interesting. (Final Iinterview, January 21, 2014)

Bridgette's intentional focus on using students' experiences and knowledge
to support their literacy development and align it to the standards of the
mainstream curriculum is what Ladson-Billings calls "counter pedagogical"
(2009, p. 30).

   Critical race theory maintains that instructional strategies supported by
the mainstream curriculum suggest that African American students are deficient (Ladson-Billings, 1994, p. 29). While bound by the state curriculum
standards, Bridgette's approach for selecting texts and writing instruction
was based on her students' experiences and knowledge.

   Bridgette experienced shifts in beliefs and practices that enabled her to
implement instruction that challenged the standardized culture of the public
education system. She was empowered to have more critical conversations
with her five-year-old students that challenged the status quo of language.
During a teacher debriefing session, she shared with the other teachers in the
study how she was able to meet the linguistic needs of her students.

Bridgette: And something that we talk about this summer, the girl that got up there, y'all remember the girl we talked about this summer, the girl from the Trayvon Martin trial? We had a long discussion about her.

Natasha: Oh yeah, umm, I can't remember her name.

Cori: You're talking about one of your students?

Bridgette: No . . . well she reminded me of my students by the way she talks.

Monica: No . . . the girl from Trayvon trial, the girl on the stand.

Cori: Oh. Yeah, yeah.

Natasha: Oh yeah, Rachel, Rachel Jeantel.

Monica: Yeah, that's it. So one of my students, one of my girls said something. We were talking about something and she said, "What's this all up in here?"

Monica: One of your kids said that?

Bridgette: Yes, and so later, we were doing something else and another student, one of my boys, said, "Ain't nobody got time for that!" So I said, OK, we have to have a conversation about this and when to talk like that and when not to talk like that. So I found this book and I shared this story [*holds up book*], *She Come Bringing Me That Little Baby Boy*, and the kids loved it, because of the same reason . . .

Cori: Because of the language?

Bridgette: Yes . . . and I explained to them there is a time to talk like this and there is nothing wrong with it and I even talk that. You'll hear me talk like that, and I said, "Ain't nobody got time for that!" I said it for the rest of the day!

[*Laughter*]

Cori: So when you had the discussion about the time and place, what was the end result? Did they understand it? I know it's kindergarten, so did they understand? OK, I have two parts: Did they understand what you said, and based on that conversation have you created a time where they can speak those ways?

Bridgette: One of our vocabulary words is "educated." So that's what I talked to them about, when to sound educated, when to talk educated and when to talk . . . and I think one of my kids yelled out, "Ghetto!" [*Interruption from announcement on the intercom*]. So to answer your question, yes, there is a time. When we are in class working you should sound educated, but when you are at centers playing you can talk like that with your friends if you want too, but there is a time and a place.

Cori: Oh, I like that. That's really good.

Morrell (2002) refers to pedagogies of access and dissent where diverse students are taught skills that differ from their everyday culture but which are necessary for them to succeed in society. However, they are also supported in developing a powerful language to critique those same systems that they are asked to navigate. Bridgette expressed her value for her students' language but engaged the students in conversations about when the language is acceptable.

Although Bridgette did not critique the system or go into detail about why code-switching is necessary in the society in which we live, her students were able to place value on their language as they learned that their teacher spoke in that way and that it did have a place in the classroom. If Bridgette had not had a space to critically examine her beliefs and negotiate assumptions, then her students may not have had a chance to consider language and see the value in theirs.

Monica's Shifts in Beliefs and Practices

At the beginning of the study, Monica believed that the students she taught were not motivated to learn. She felt that she had to work twice as hard to educate students because their parents had not instilled in them the importance of education. Monica attributed her students' lack of academic success to having parents who did not care about their children's education.

Research on attribution theories reveals that the way teachers perceive students impacts their ability to meet students' instructional needs (Raths, 2001). When teachers attribute students' lack of success to factors other than teaching, such as lack of parental support or home life, adequate teaching and learning cannot take place (Raths, 2001).

The professional learning provided a space for Monica to reflect on her beliefs and consider how what she viewed as deficits in her students were the result of historical and societal factors that marginalized people of color. In a discussion during the professional learning sessions that were held in the summer, Monica expressed the difficulty she had with parents who did not know and did not try to find information that could benefit their child. Carolyn used an analogy about slavery to explain it to her.

Monica: As far as you saying they may not know, I just, I can't accept that, because I don't know how to fix a toilet, but if I want to learn, I'll Google it. I'm thinking if you want your kid to be successful, even if you don't know yourself, why can't you say to the teacher. . . .

Carolyn: That's a big *if* baby!

Samantha: But, but at the same time. . . .

Carolyn: Your parents passed that belief on to you. But you know I always go back. Our history in our country is skewed through the eyes of what they said was good . . . bad . . . success . . . failure. It's like, the people, those that worked in the big house serving the master and guests, they had a mindset of being better than the masses who was in the fields. I'm just saying that the majority of us was out there in the fields; they didn't have no belief and no hope that something was going to get better. They just had to pick cotton and do what whatever, that was in their mind. Those in the big house got to read, got to present, they got to see a better life. (Day 3 of professional development, July 18, 2013)

Carolyn's point was to show that lack of knowledge about education was systemic and reproduced in society starting with slavery. During another discussion on language use, the teachers read sections of "The Real Ebonics Debate" by Lisa Delpit and a synopsis of Shirley Brice Heaths's study "Ways with Words" about oral language development among various communities of people.

I wanted the teachers to gain a broader understanding of language use and to think more critically about how they can acknowledge and build on it in their classrooms. The following day we continued our discussion about language, and I shared a quote by James Gee with the participants: "All children have impressive language abilities." Aside from Carolyn, the other participants had not known about these studies and the research in these areas. The quote challenged their thinking and pushed them to engage in topics they had not discussed before:

Natasha: Do you all agree?

[*Carolyn and Samantha nod their heads.*]

Monica: Well. . . .

Natasha: What?

Monica: Nothing. Go ahead.

Carolyn: I mean, what schools mean by large vocabularies and complex grammar may be different from what we understand and different from what the children bring. Like Heath was saying, the children from Trackton knew how to talk and they knew what each other was saying, but some Caucasian teachers may be like "What are they talking about?"

Bridgette: Some black teachers too.

Natasha: Yeah, some black too.

[*Heads nod.*]

Cori: Me!

[*Laughter*]

Carolyn: Yeah, some Black too, so what we have to understand, what they say is complex or large vocabulary, it may be a cultural vocabulary.

Bridgette: I agree with it if that's what he's saying.

Carolyn: If we were to take them to the hood, then. . . .

Natasha: Just knowing our students have experiences, they may not have certain experiences but the experiences they have are valuable because they are theirs.

Bridgette: That's interesting.

Samantha: What's interesting?

Bridgette: Just the large vocabulary, just thinking about it like that.

Samantha: Yeah it is, or even the impressive language abilities, I was about to be like "uh unh."

[*Laughter*]

Samantha: And when you look at . . . that's what I'm . . . I don't know if I want to say I'm struggling, but . . .

Natasha: That's fine, we all struggle with . . .

Samantha: That's going to be a struggle for me to look at it from a different angle, and I think it's because I don't . . . the most, most of the time the way I speak is Standard English. So to think that BEV could be standard is like, huh? That's something that I am working on.

Carolyn: Because we are standardized by teacher education programs, we are standardized, when you go through teacher education programs it's an enculturation too usually, not an enculturation with a proclivity to people like us.

Monica: So, yeah, that's kind of where I am.

Natasha: Yeah, and that's the point of all of this. . . . I'm still pushing myself.

Samantha: And I think that handout you gave us Tuesday with the Track-ton and the . . .

Natasha: Yeah . . .

Samantha: I think that's why when I first read that [*pointing to quote*] I was like, yeah, I agree, and that was the first thing that I thought about different cultures and yes, how they have impressive language abilities you know based off their understandings and culture, so that's what I immediately thought about, so, yeah, I agree.

Monica: So you all already changed.

[*Laughter*]

Samantha: That's where my mind first went to now that I have been exposed to it. (Day 3 of professional development, July 18, 2013)

This exchange demonstrates how the teachers began to work through and problematize some long-standing beliefs about language use and cultural deficit models when presented with theory-driven professional development. Carolyn, already knowledgeable about cultural studies, was able to help Monica understand the lens through which she viewed language by discussing the enculturation of teacher education programs.

For Samantha, the research that she read helped her understand the value in the languages that her students used; Monica struggled with this new information but could begin to see how it made sense. In an interview after the professional development, Monica discussed how the conversation and the articles they read "kind of pushed our thinking a little bit" (Post–professional development interview, July 30, 2013).

Once school began, Monica had difficulties framing her instruction in culturally relevant ways. She saw cultural relevance as interrupting the teaching of the standards rather than enhancing the students' ability to learn the standards. She wanted to revise the structure of her literacy block to offer students a choice in reading materials so that reading instruction would become relevant and individualized. However, lack of time and adherence to the curriculum pacing chart caused Monica to have difficulties:

> I know time is a constraint when it comes to culturally relevant pedagogy. It's time in planning too, because I do not put the time into it as I should to intentionally think of culturally relevant plans. It's easier to pull the textbook and say read this and then you know that standard is covered. Now I don't mind doing things that directly connect to what I am teaching, but it takes more time to plan for that too. (Teacher debriefing session, October 10, 2013)

During the continuous, in-class support of the professional development, Monica planned to effectively integrate her reading and social studies content, as she saw that the lack of time inhibited her ability to cover all of the instructional standards. Along with the researcher, Monica developed a socio-critical lesson plan in which she integrated a reading and social studies lesson.

These modifications to her previous instruction allowed her to provide students multiple engagements with self-selected texts and provided a platform to teach from a critical stance while integrating reading and social studies standards. The social studies standards addressed explorers, so Monica designed a lesson around Christopher Columbus. Various texts about Columbus were used, and the students read and responded to the texts during a two-hour block that combined the allotted time for both subjects.

Monica read *The Encounter* by Jane Yolen, which offers the perspective of the Taino people who were living in San Salvador when Columbus claimed it for Spain. Students read and discussed a textbook passage from a critical perspective by asking more questions. Monica began to have more discussions with her students on various topics that were currently in the news and that the students could connect to. She talked about the government shutdown and two high-profile cases that centered on race.

Monica noticed that her students were more involved during these discussions. She believed that she saw increased engagement in class discussions because these discussions did not necessarily warrant right or wrong answers but were based on students' beliefs and experiences. When Monica began to look for multiple texts to increase students' reading in social studies, she began to notice bias in the curriculum and wanted to open up these conversations with her fourth-grade students.

Examining the curriculum and assignments for bias allows teachers to bring in multiple perspectives and reconstruct discussions around critical and inclusive topics (Kesler, 2011). During Monica's last interview, she referenced the discussions during our four-day professional development and debriefing sessions about using topics the students are learning about in class, saying, "I empathize with my students now that I have a more understanding of, like, how history affects their backgrounds and experience. So it is important to have these critical conversations with them" (Final interview, January 23, 2014). She continued by sharing how she believed that having critical conversations with her students increases their engagement in school and brings attention to inequities in society so that "their fight will be all the bit more."

IMPLICATIONS FOR PRACTITIONERS

The teachers' shifting process described in this chapter illustrate that learning about and implementing culturally relevant pedagogy is a complex process and requires being thoughtful and intentional. The hope, however, is that it is not a daunting process but rather one that can be enhanced by various factors from which teachers can learn.

During the study, teachers faced issues with time, instructional standards, and lack of support—things that many teachers deal with in some way. However, a detailed description of how each teacher became more intentional in her implementation of CRP motivate others. Teachers interested in culturally relevant pedagogy must consider actions and activities that support implementing CRP in meaningful ways.

Based on the findings and discussion from this study, teachers should (1) develop communities of practice and work with colleagues that have similar goals for learning, (2) spend time reading, discussing, and reflecting on the theoretical tenets of CRP, and (3) continuously support one other during their processes.

CONCLUSION

Much of the literature on culturally relevant pedagogy notes the difficulties that teachers have when implementing CRP even when knowledgeable and passionate about supporting culturally and linguistically diverse students (Esposito and Swain, 2009; May, 2011; Rozansky, 2010). Teachers who implement culturally relevant practices are needed to critically examine their own beliefs as well as inequities in education.

However, teachers need spaces to dialogue and negotiate their beliefs in order to become culturally relevant teachers who implement practices that support the development of all students. One important shift in teachers' beliefs in this study was that they more fully understood that students bring to the classroom a range of experiences and knowledge that can be used as a catalyst for curriculum and learning.

All of the teachers saw their students' experiences and language in more positive ways. Bridgette valued individual students' experiences, whereas Monica empathized with children's family lives and backgrounds, leading her to discuss sociopolitical factors with students. Although the teachers did experience positive shifts in beliefs and practices, during the process they were still negotiating beliefs about the students they taught and their families.

Beliefs and practices inform each other as they are developed and practiced. Though the shifts in teachers' beliefs may be small, awareness of beliefs and the need to change to teach students more effectively is necessary. Furthermore, the shifts that the teachers experienced during this study are likely to continue to shape their beliefs and practices for years to come.

REFERENCES

Allington, R. L. (2002). What I've learned about effective reading instruction from a decade of studying exemplary elementary classroom teachers. *Phi Delta Kappan*, 83(10), 740–47.

Au, K. H. (1998). Social constructivism and the school literacy learning of students of diverse backgrounds. *Journal of Literacy Research*, 30, 297–319.

Au, K. H., and Jordan, C. (1981). Teaching reading to Hawaiian children: Finding a culturally appropriate solution. In H. Trueba, G. Guthrie, and K. H. Au (Eds.), *Culture and the bilingual classroom: Studies in classroom ethnography* (139–152). Rowley, MA: Newbury House.

Banks, J. A. (2004). *Multicultural education: Historical development, dimensions, and practice*. In J. A. Banks and C. A. McGee Banks (Eds.), *Handbook of research on multicultural education*, second edition (3–29). San Francisco: Jossey-Bass.

Birchak, B., Connor, C., Crawford, K., Kahn, L., Kaser, S., Turner, S., and Short, K. (1998). *Teacher study groups: Building community through dialogue and reflection*. Urbana, IL: National Council of Teachers of English.

Clair, N. (1993). ESL teacher educators and teachers: Insights from classroom teachers with language-minority students. Presentation at the annual meeting of the Teachers of English to Speakers of Other Languages, Atlanta, GA.

Delpit, L. (2006). *Other people's children: Cultural conflict in the classroom*. New York: New Press.

Esposito, J., and Swain, A. N. (2009). Pathways to social justice: Urban teachers' uses of culturally relevant pedagogy as a conduit for teaching for social justice. *Perspectives on Urban Education*, Spring, 38–48.

Gay, G. (2002). Preparing for culturally relevant teaching. *Journal of Teacher Education*, 53 (2), 106–16.

Green, L. (2002). A descriptive study of African American English: Research in linguistics and education. *Qualitative Studies in Education*, 15(6), 673–90.

Gupta, A. (2010). African-American English: Teacher beliefs, teacher needs and teacher preparation programs. *Reading Matrix: An International Online Journal*, 10(2), 152–64.

Johnson, A. (1995). *Shoes like Miss Alice's*. New York: Orchard Books.

Kavanagh, K. M. (2010). A dichotomy examined: Beginning Teach for America educators navigate culturally relevant teaching and a scripted literacy program in their urban classrooms. Georgia State University, Early Childhood Education Dissertations 12. Retrieved from http://digitalarchive.gsu.edu/ece_diss/12.

Kena, G., Aud, S., Johnson, F., Wang, X., Zhang, J., Rathbun, A., Wilkinson-Flicker, S., and Kristapovich, P. (2014). The Condition of Education 2014 (NCES 2014-083). U.S. Department of Education. Washington, DC: National Center for Education Statistics.

Kesler, T. (2011). Teachers' texts in culturally responsive teaching. *Language Arts*, 88(6), 419–28.

Kincheloe, J. L., and McLaren, P. (2002). Rethinking critical theory and qualitative research. In Yali Zou and Enrique T. Trueba (Eds.), *Ethnography and schools: Qualitative approaches to the study of education*. Lanham, MD: Rowman and Littlefield.

Knight, S. L., and Wiseman, D. L. (2005). Professional development for teachers of diverse students: A summary of the research. *Journal of Education for Students Placed at Risk*, 10(4), 387–405.

Kuzborska, I. (2011). Links between teachers' beliefs and practices and research on reading. *Reading in a Foreign Language*, 23(1), 103–29.

Ladson-Billings, G. (1994). *The dreamkeepers: Successful teachers of African-American children*. San Francisco: Jossey-Bass.

Ladson-Billings, G. (2009). Just what is critical race theory and what's it doing in a nice field like education? In E. Taylor, D. Gilborn, and G. Ladson-Billings (Eds.), *Critical race theory in education* (17–36). New York: Routledge.

Lazar, A. M., Edwards, P. A., and McMillon, G. T. (2012). *Bridging literacy and equity: The essential guide to social equity teaching*. New York: Teachers College Press.

Lee, C. D. (2007). *Culture, literacy and learning: Taking bloom in the midst of the whirlwind*. New York: Teachers College Press.

May, L. A. (2011). Situating strategies: An examination of comprehension strategy instruction in one upper elementary classroom oriented towards culturally relevant teaching. *Literacy Research and Instruction*, 50(1), 31–42.

Merriam, S. B. (2009). *Qualitative research: A guide to design and implementation*. San Francisco: CA: Jossey-Bass.

Milner, H. R. (2009). Preparing teachers of African American students urban schools. In L. C. Tillman (Ed.), *The sage handbook of African American education* (123–39). Thousand Oaks, CA: Sage.

Milner, H. R. (2011). Culturally relevant pedagogy in a diverse urban classroom. *Urban Review*, 43(1), 66–89.

Mohatt, C., and Erickson, F. (1982). Cultural differences in teaching studies in Odawa School: A sociolinguistic approach. In H. Trueba, G. Guthrie, and K. Au (Eds.), *Culture and the bilingual classroom: Studies in classroom ethnography* (105–19). Rowley, MA: Newbury House.

Moll, L. C., Armanti, C., Neff, D., and Gonzalez, N. (1992). Funds of knowledge for teaching: Using a qualitative approach to connect homes and classrooms. *Theory into Practice*, 31(2), 132–41.

Morrell, E. (2002). Toward a critical pedagogy of popular culture: Implications for academic and critical literacy development among urban youth. *Journal of Adolescent and Adult Literacy*, 46(1), 72–77.

Nieto, S. (April 2009). Cuentos that matter: The messages of Latino children's literature. Keynote presentation at the Latino children's literature conference, Columbia, SC.

Paris, D. (2012). Culturally sustaining pedagogy: A needed change in stance, terminology, and practice. *Educational Researcher*, 41(3), 93–97.

Patton, D. C. (2011). Evaluating the culturally relevant and responsive education professional development program at the elementary school level in the Los Angeles Unified School District. *Learning Disabilities*, 9(1), 71–107.

Perry, T. (1997). Reflections on the Ebonics debate. *Rethinking Schools*. Retrieved from http://www.rethinkingschools.org/publication/ebonics/ebperry.shtml.

Powers, S. W., Zippay, C., and Butler, B. (2006). Investigating connections between teacher beliefs and instructional practices with struggling readers. *Reading Horizon Journal*, 47(2), 121–57.

Raths, J. (2001). Teachers' beliefs and teaching beliefs. *Early Childhood Research and Practice*, (3)1.

Richardson, V., Anders, P., Tidwell, D., and Lloyd, C. (1991). The relationship between teachers' beliefs and practices in reading comprehension instruction. *American Educational Research Journal*, 28(3), 559–86.

Rozansky, C. L. (2010). A bumpy journey to culturally relevant pedagogy in an urban middle school: Are we there yet? *Journal of Urban Learning, Teaching, and Research*, 6, 1–13.

Smitherman, G. (2006). *Word from the mother: Language and African Americans*. New York: Routledge.

Souto-Manning, M., and Price-Dennis, D. (2012). Critically redefining and repositioning media texts in early childhood teacher education: What if? and why? *Journal of Early Childhood Teacher Education*, 33(4).

Villegas, A. and Lucas, T. (2007). The culturally responsive teacher. *Educational Leadership*, 64(6), 28–33.

Wynter-Hoyte, K. (2014). The Black middle class: Negotiating literacy identities in church and school. Dissertation, Georgia State University. Retrieved from http://scholarworks.gsu.edu/msit_diss/137.

III

Bridging Literacy and the Community

Chapter Seven

Summer Bridge Programs to Encourage Literacy Success for All Children

Megan Adams, Kate Zimmer, and Sanjuana Rodriguez

Introduction Classroom Example: Connecting with Kids

The undergraduate teacher candidates sit in a group debating how to deliver the qualitative reading assessments to their students. One turns to the group and says, "My student is reading above grade level. What do you do with a third grader reading at a sixth-grade level?" The others murmur in response. One says, "I thought this program was for kids who couldn't read?"

There are some discussions of this. Another says, "Don't say that. They can read; they are performing below grade level." The first candidate responds, "The point is that mine is above grade level!" Finally, they call a professor to come over and assist. "Dr. Adams, what are we supposed to do? These kids are all on different performance levels!" Dr. Adams replies, "Welcome to a typical classroom."

The candidates decide to continue their discussion in their regular class meeting. Additional strategies seem to be needed to meet the needs of each student. They comment as they leave to tutor that this is only a summer program; they ponder in the hallway what will happen when they have to do this alone for a room full of twenty children.

BRIDGE PROGRAMS AS FIELD EXPERIENCES

Teacher preparation programs often find it difficult to provide teacher candidates with meaningful P–12 field experiences during the summer months. In times of budget cuts, school districts are often unable to provide summer programs that focus on developing skills in reading. Furthermore, at the end of the school year local education agencies (LEAs) often have learners who have not met adequately yearly progress across content areas and have few funds to provide additional assistance.

Summer literacy and bridge programs are important to fill the gap left by these problems. Our team set out to create a summer literacy program that would allow students in P–12 schools to develop their literacy while also providing a summer field experience for our undergraduate teaching candidates pursuing a degree in elementary and early childhood education.

The literacy summer program for students lasted from 8:30 a.m. to 3:30 p.m. each day. A field experience for undergraduate students typically requires twenty hours over the course of a semester. Therefore, in order to provide a meaningful experience for the students participating in the summer program, it was necessary to hire tutors who were with the P–12 students for the full day while also offering field experiences to literacy "experts" who would work with children for a few hours each week.

This created a layered approach where each college student who participated had a role to play that was integral to the success of the program for the P–12 children. To assist readers in understanding the terms used in the chapter, we have provided the following definitions:

- *Student.* A P–12 student from a public school attending the summer program.
- *Teaching candidate.* A college student enrolled in an undergraduate literacy instruction and assessment course during the summer; the field experience involved tutoring students enrolled in the summer program.
- *Tutor.* A college student hired using America Reads funding to work on various aspects of literacy (content area or disciplinary literacy) throughout the full day of the camp.
- *Lead teacher.* One of two teachers hired to develop curriculum; both were recommended by at least two college professors and had completed all coursework for a degree in elementary and early childhood education.

This chapter explains how one summer literacy program was created, how meaningful partnerships were built, how all parties benefited, and how such a framework can be successfully replicated.

THE PERFECT STORM: HOW DO YOU KNOW IF IMPLEMENTING A SUMMER LITERACY PROGRAM IS RIGHT FOR YOU?

When a literacy center is located in a suburban area, it provides the perfect setting to reach students who are in need of additional reading support or are performing below grade level. This support, whether provided through a summer reading program, tutoring sessions, intensive interventions, or a combination, enhances student achievement, provides teacher candidates the opportunity to practice, and allows teachers to hone their pedagogical skills.

STEP 1: CREATE A NEEDS ASSESSMENT

An existing outreach program approached the reading faculty at a southeastern university to determine if the college of education would be interested in taking over an extant summer literacy program. The program was funded by America Reads for students entering third through fifth grade who were performing below grade level in reading. The outreach program could no longer support such a project because of a lack of staffing and the reorganization of duties and responsibilities across several units.

The reading faculty knew that both their teacher candidates and the third- through fifth-grade students could have a meaningful experience through embedding a summer literacy program in the college's summer literacy assessment course. But before taking on such a project, faculty wanted to be thoughtful and purposeful in the design and implementation of the program. They posed two overarching questions:

1. Do we have the need in our community at the local and college level?
2. What does a successful literacy tutoring program look like?

The faculty also interviewed former employees, students, their parents or guardians, and the former director to gather information on the successes and challenges of the existing program.

The first research question was an easy one to answer—yes! The reading faculty knew that both their teacher candidates and the outreach students could have a meaningful experience through embedding a summer literacy program into the college. In a large suburban area, there were many schools with students needing assistance. The former director and parents and guardians responded that they would very much like the program to continue, confirming what the local school districts said.

The second question was a bit more complex. Researchers decided that in order to implement a quality summer literacy program they would review the literature on how successful reading programs function.

STEP 2: REVIEW THE LITERATURE ON SUCCESSFUL LITERACY TUTORING PROGRAMS

The reading faculty started researching programs like America Reads that aim to increase literacy achievement of students with low socioeconomic status. America Reads was started by President Bill Clinton in 1996 as part of a national literacy campaign whose aim was to have "one million volunteer tutors ready and able to give children the personal attention they need to catch up and get ahead" (www.americareads.as.ucsb.edu, 2016). Congress approved the use of federal work-study funds to have college students tutor children in kindergarten through sixth grade.

Elements of Successful Programs

The literature review provided the reading faculty a variety of successful elements and evidence-based practices common throughout successful reading programs, as described below.

- Literacy tutoring work should be conducted with diverse students to best impact student achievement and allow the growth of preservice teachers in reaching all students (Kim and Warren, 2013; Wasik, 1998). Recruiting students performing below grade level in reading and those who receive free or reduced-price lunch did not guarantee racial diversity; however, these criteria generated a pool of culturally diverse students. This was important to meet the goal of providing a diverse field experience for the teaching candidates; nearly all of the candidates were white females from predominantly middle-class backgrounds, which was typical of the candidates in this college of education.
- Initial reviews of literature found disappointing lists and resources aimed only at volunteers working with students from diverse backgrounds (Arendale, 2015; Washington State, 1994). The tutors in the America Reads program are not volunteers; they are paid to work with students from the community. While the mission of the Center for Literacy and Learning (CLL) does not distinguish between paid tutoring and volunteer work, the directors felt it important to hold the paid tutors to a set of measurable goals for their work.
- For the teacher candidates working with children on literacy, the resources were somewhat more helpful. Programs like Reading Rockets provide lists of summer texts for students; the CLL also has a library for students to choose age-appropriate texts.
- Immediately following the implementation of America Reads, numerous studies were conducted to investigate the ability of college students to impact the reading ability of K–12 students (Kim and Warren, 2013). Those studies often investigated the best practices for increasing reading achievement (Fitzgerald, 2001; Kim and Warren, 2013).
- The "7 strengths model" provides insight into using students' strengths to build a "super reader." The strengths are "belonging," "curiosity," "friendship," "kindness," "confidence," "courage," and "hope" (Allyn and Morrell, 2016, pp. 32–36), and they are common in literature on culturally

relevant pedagogy as a tool to reach all students (Alvermann et al., 2006; Ladson-Billings, 1995b).

Evidence-Based Practices

The literature on reading remediation indicates that students should be taught using evidence-based strategies to ensure that struggling readers are learning the skills necessary to grow (Hougen, 2014; Lane, 2014). The following bullets highlight those best practices, and the text below each bulleted item explains how they were implemented within the summer reading program:

- Frequent opportunity to practice literacy skills (Gaskins et al., 1997; Gettinger and Seibert, 2002; Greenwood et al., 1994; Power et al., 2004).

Students worked with tutors daily on their literacy skills. The curriculum was approved by the directors of the CLL before implementation; it was structured appropriately for all learners. The day began with journal writing on the text being read by each child. This activity was followed by either reading circles or reading instruction (as days varied for the teaching candidates).

A midmorning snack allowed students to spend time with each other and with the teacher candidate in a relaxed setting. The late morning was dedicated to literacy games, followed by a lunch break. Early afternoon allowed the students to focus on literacy projects in class; the theme chosen was entrepreneurship. There were guest speakers and computer research each afternoon; a project-based learning model was implemented for this component.

- The opportunity to respond to instruction (Gaskins et al., 1997; Gettinger and Seibert, 2002; Greenwood et al., 1994; Power et al., 2004).

The lead teachers and tutors were able to interact daily with students, which allowed the camp to run more like a traditional third-grade classroom. The tutoring functioned as tutoring often does; the teaching candidates gave children the opportunity to respond to instruction several times per week.

This worked quite well; teaching candidates responded that they were making great gains by having time to reflect during the instruction and assessment cycle. The tutors and lead teachers learned a great deal as well; they asked questions like, "What do we do when we don't have the help of the tutors?" The direction of the faculty involved allowed them to process how this would work in a "typical" classroom. The project-based learning opportunity appealed to them because it allowed for more one-on-one interaction and differentiation.

- Providing a supportive environment where attachments can be formed (Gaskins et al., 1997; Gettinger and Seibert, 2002; Greenwood et al., 1994; Power et al., 2004).

A satisfaction survey was offered to all parents and guardians involved in this iteration of the program. In the table below, the survey questions and responses are recorded. This was a Likert survey; parents were asked to rate on a scale of 1 (strongly negative) to 5 (strongly positive). The rate of response is calculated by the total respondents; the survey was sent out to twenty parents and guardians who provided e-mail addresses. Only five of the twenty, or 25 percent, responded to the survey. There were also four open-ended questions on the survey.

1. If your child needs individual tutoring, would you be willing to extend the duration of the camp to three weeks? Why or why not?
2. We have considered a three-week elementary program and a two-week program for middle grades children. Do you have or know middle grades children who would benefit from a similar experience?
3. We are always looking to make improvements to our programs. Do you have suggestions for future summer programs?
4. Would you be willing to recommend the program to a friend? Please briefly explain why or why not.

Parents responded to all four questions in favorable ways. Some comments were that "exposure to a college campus is nice," "the program gives kids the opportunity to learn in a smaller space," "we love the program and would be happy to come back," and "this program is genius." The only constructive criticism was to increase the focus on math comprehension, which is under advisement for future summers.

- Successful literacy tutoring programs require "teaching the right skills . . . using the right materials, with the right intensity or frequency, in the right learning environments, with the right people" (Power et al., 2004, p. 95).

In a previous iteration of this program, the researchers worked with the former director to study the impact of tutoring on the preservice teaching candidates' sense of efficacy. The researchers found that the candidates felt an increased sense of efficacy after working with students performing below grade level in reading (Rodriguez, Adams, and Zimmer, 2016).

The results also found areas, such as classroom management, where teaching candidates were not seeing an increased sense of efficacy. For this iteration of the summer camp, the researchers shifted responsibility to the tutors, who were establishing more direct supervisory relationships with the

Table 7.1. Survey for Parents and Guardians

Question	Response	Rate of response
How satisfied were you with the camp activities?	40% satisfied 60% very satisfied	100%
Were the camp staff courteous?	40% satisfied 60% very satisfied	100%
How happy were you with the ease of the registration process?	100% very satisfied	100%
How happy were you with the emphasis on reading?	40% neither satisfied nor dissatisfied 20% satisfied 40% very satisfied	100%
How happy were you with the tutoring / one-to-one learning?	60% satisfied 40% very satisfied	100%
How happy were you with the games / active learning?	40% neither satisfied nor dissatisfied 20% satisfied 40% very satisfied	100%

students. The tutors were only working with children in a more structured, supervised environment.

STEP 3: FIND FUNDING

In our university, America Reads pays for reading tutoring and reading programs throughout the school year. In 2000, every institution of higher education that received federal work-study funds was mandated to have a literacy tutoring program, and 7 percent of the funds had to be spent on community outreach or service (U.S. Department of Education, 2016).

> Institutions must use at least 7 percent of their work-study allocation to support students working in community service jobs, including: reading tutors for preschool age or elementary school children; mathematics tutors for students enrolled in elementary school through ninth grade; literacy tutors in a family literacy project performing family literacy activities; or emergency preparedness and response. (U. S. Department of Education, 2016)

The office handling funding, such as the office of financial aid, is a good place to start for university groups seeking to fund a summer literacy program. Hiring students through federal work-study is another potential avenue for faculty beginning literacy programs. While other small grants are often available, the current national push for STEM work seems to have shifted the funding landscape (Kruenzi, 2008). In lieu of private donors, it is often advisable to look at state funding.

In many states, funds for Title I schools may be spent on summer programs. School districts in our area were willing to discuss using those funds for summer programs; community members wanting to begin literacy programs may want to approach the local board of education first. There are summer programs at most local libraries and YMCAs; those are other valuable resources for implementing literacy programs connecting the community and K–12 students.

Finally, many states still have grants like Striving Readers that have budgets for summer or afterschool literacy programs. Investigating the needs of local districts is helpful in establishing those possibilities. Finally, the Youth Today program has valuable resources for best practices in afterschool programs; they often link to websites funding afterschool initiatives (www.youthtoday.org).

STEP 4: ESTABLISH PARTNERSHIPS

When we knew that we would be able to provide the summer tutoring program to teacher candidates, we had to make a decision about what courses we could tie to the program. The Literacy Assessment course is typically offered in the summer to our undergraduate students in elementary education. This course includes a twenty-hour field experience.

We have had difficulty finding field experience placements for this course because schools are not in session in the summer and the course requires tutoring a student one on one. During the twenty-hour experience, teacher candidates have to complete an informal reading inventory (usually the QRI-5) and other assessments including a spelling inventory, writing sample, and any other appropriate assessments. Based on these assessments, teacher candidates develop instructional plans that are then implemented with the student.

One of the course objectives states that the teacher candidate will "understand literacy assessment and instructional approaches that support all learners, including struggling readers, English language learners, students from a variety of cultural backgrounds, and those with special needs."

The Fast Start Academy provided the opportunity for teacher candidates to work with students from culturally and linguistically diverse backgrounds. Teacher candidates in our program are able to request placements and may or may not have the opportunity to work with students from diverse backgrounds; thus, this course allowed teacher candidates who participated at Fast Start to have this experience.

STEP 5: TRAIN THE TUTORS

One essential task was to ensure that the tutoring was helpful for the teacher candidates, the paid tutors in the program, and the students, and we had distinct goals for each group. The goal for the paid tutors and teachers was to provide them additional experiences working with diverse students. Most of these students were going to complete their student teaching the following semester; thus, this provided another experience before student teaching to practice what they had learned in their courses.

Our goal for the teacher candidates was for them to learn about literacy assessments. We also wanted the teacher candidates to work with students from diverse backgrounds. The goal for the young students was for them to have a positive literacy experience coupled with one-to-one tutoring.

Another task was to acclimate the paid tutors and lead teachers to the program and provide them with the expectations. Most of the paid tutors and both lead teachers were part of our elementary education program and thus had some experience working with young children. These tutors and lead teachers were all undergraduate students, though most were nearing the end of their program.

The lead teachers began to work two weeks prior to the start of the program. At an initial meeting, they were given the description of the program and were able to look at some notebooks that chronicled the program and materials used in the program. The two lead teachers were tasked with designing the curriculum they would use for Fast Start Academy and with planning a training session for the paid tutors for the program, both of which were evaluated and approved by the CLL directors. At the training for the tutors, one of directors for the program was able to discuss the goals for the program and procedures.

The teacher candidates that were in the literacy assessment course also needed preparation time. The course took place in the summer for eight weeks. Fast Start Academy began during the third week of the course. The timing of the course and the Fast Start Academy required significant front-loading in order to prepare the teacher candidates to administer and analyze assessments, plan for instruction, and prepare for their lessons.

Teacher candidates knew this ahead of time and understood the process. The first two weeks of the course were devoted to intensive instruction focused on assessments. Informal reading inventories were introduced, and students practiced giving and scoring the Qualitative Reading Inventory-5 (Leslie and Caldwell, 2011). Teacher candidates also learned how to get to know students' personal, family, and community assets. Teacher candidates were required to give "Child's Concept of Reading" (Owocki and Goodman, 2002) the first time they met with their tutee.

In addition to this, teacher candidates had to send home a questionnaire that would help them learn more about the student they were working with, with the goal of using this information as they were planning their lessons.

When the tutoring began it was important that the teacher candidates had someone available to answer their questions. For most of the teacher candidates, this was the first time they were administering an informal reading inventory, and they had many questions. The directors, who were both literacy faculty, provided support as they made decisions about the assessments. Students also came back together after the tutoring sessions to debrief and to ask additional questions.

STEP 6: INVOLVE FAMILIES IN THE PROGRAM

One of the goals of any effective literacy program is to engage families in the literacy work that their children are experiencing. We knew from past years that parents had successfully participated in this program in different ways. The first step that we took to introduce ourselves to the families was to have an initial meeting. Our goal was to build trust and to help them understand the transition in program directors.

We also wanted to help the parents understand changes in the structures and procedures of the program. We needed a full commitment from the parents to provide transportation every day for the students. We also needed a commitment for continued attendance in the program. Parents communicated on a regular basis with the program directors, the lead teachers, and the tutors who assisted in the program.

All of the parents received a questionnaire from the lead teachers with questions about their household. The goal was to help the lead teachers understand the funds of knowledge that students had in their homes (González, Moll, and Amanti, 2005). The lead teachers also created an e-mail list used to send reminders to parents on a regular basis. The lead teachers were consistent in sending all communication to parents in English and Spanish.

CONCLUSION: LESSONS LEARNED

We learned some lessons learned and intend to implement some changes moving forward. First, we plan to have a more extensive orientation for the lead teachers and tutors to explain in greater detail the expectation for the program and roles and responsibilities. We believe this would have prevented some of the misunderstandings about the role of the paid tutors versus the role of the lead teachers. For example, it is important for the tutors to take an active role even during times the lead teachers are doing most of the teaching.

The tutors could sit with individual students, work with small groups, or assist the lead teacher with instruction. This was not clear, and tutors were often disengaged or attending to tasks not related to instruction. It is also important for the paid tutors to attend the initial meeting with the parents. During this meeting, we discussed the program, the expectations for students and parents, and safety procedures. The tutors would have benefited from having this information.

Overall, the Fast Start literacy-tutoring program was a great success for all stakeholders. It is important that we provide our teacher candidates with the opportunity to practice important literacy skills with diverse students. Preparing our teacher candidates while providing a valuable resource during the summer months for the community is important work. This chapter may provide a useful roadmap for other institutions of higher education and community organizations hoping to increase summer literacy bridge work.

REFERENCES

Allyn, P., and Morrell, E. (2016). *Every child a super reader: 7 strengths to open a world of possible.* New York: Scholastic.

Alvermann, D. E., Hinchman, K. A., Moore, D. W., Phelps, S. P., and Waff, D. R. (Eds.). (2006). *Reconceptualizing the literacies in adolescents' lives.* Second edition. Mahwah, NJ: Lawrence Erlbaum.

America Reads. (2016). About us. Retrieved from https://americareads.as.ucsb.edu/about-us/.

Arendale, D. R. (2015). *MAEPOPP Center 2015 best practices directory.* Minneapolis: Mid-America Association for Educational Opportunity Program Personnel and University of Minnesota. Retrieved from http://www.eric.ed.gov/contentdelivery/servlet/ERICServlet?accno=ED557575.

Bandura, A. (1997). *Self-efficacy: The exercise of control.* New York: W. H. Freeman.

Fitzgerald, J. (2001). Can minimally trained college student volunteers help young at-risk children to read better? *Reading Research Quarterly,* 36(1), 28–46.

Gaskins, I. W., Ehri, L. C., Cress, C., O'Hara, C., and Donnelly, K. (1997). Procedures for word learning: Making discoveries about words. *Reading Teacher,* 50, 312–27.

Gettinger, M., and Seibert, J. K. (2002). Best practices in increasing academic learning time. In A. Thomas and J. Grimes (Eds.), *Best practices in school psychology IV* (773–88). Bethesda, MD: National Association of School Psychologists.

González, N., Moll, L. C., and Amanti, C. (Eds.). (2005). *Funds of knowledge: Theorizing practices in households, communities, and classrooms.* New York: Routledge.

Greenwood, C. R., Terry, B., Marquis, J. and Walker, D. (1994). Confirming a performance-based instructional model. *School Psychology Review,* 23, 652–68.

Hougen, M. (2015). *Evidence-based reading instruction for adolescents, grades 6–12.* Document IC-13. Retrieved from University of Florida, Collaboration for Effective Educator, Development, Accountability, and Reform Center website: http://ceedar.education.ufl.edu/tools/innovation-configurations.

Kim, S. C., and Warren, S. (2013). Making connections: Preparing college tutors to support the literacy of urban children. *Journal of Urban Learning, Teaching, and Research,* 9, 124–37.

Kruenzi, J. (2008). *Science, technology, engineering, and mathematics (STEM) education: Background, federal policy, and legislative action.* Washington, DC: Congressional Research Service. Retrieved from http://www.fas.org/ sgp/crs/misc/RL33434.pdf.

Ladson-Billings, G. (1995b). Toward a theory of culturally relevant pedagogy. *American Educational Research Journal*, 32(3), 455–61.

Lane, H. (2014). *Evidence-based reading instruction for grades K–5.* Document IC-12. Retrieved from University of Florida, Collaboration for Effective Educator, Development, Accountability, and Reform Center website: http://ceedar.education.ufl.edu/tools/innovation-configurations.

Leslie, L., and Caldwell, J. A. (2011). *Qualitative reading inventory: 5.* Boston: Pearson/Allyn and Bacon.

Morrow, L. M., and Woo, D. G. (2001). *Tutoring programs for struggling readers: The America Reads challenge.* New York: Guilford.

Ornstein, A. C., Pajak, E. F., and Ornstein, S. B. (Eds.) (2011). *Contemporary issues in curriculum.* Fifth edition. Boston: Pearson.

Owocki, G., and Goodman, Y. (2002). *Kidwatching: Documenting children's literacy development.* Westport, CT: Heinemann.

Power, T. J., Dowrick, P. W., Ginsburg-Block, M., and Manz, P. H. (2004). Partnership-based, community-assisted early intervention for literacy: An application of the participatory intervention model. *Journal of Behavioral Education*, 13(2), 93–115.

Rodriguez, S., Adams, M. G., and Zimmer, K. A. (2016). Fostering diverse praxis: How work in a diverse setting impacts pre-service teachers' perceptions of efficacy. In C. Martin and D. Polly (Eds.), *Handbook of Teacher Education and Professional Development.* Hershey, PA: IGI Global.

Tschannen-Moran, M. and Johnson, D. (2011). Exploring literacy teachers' self-efficacy beliefs: Potential sources at play. *Teaching and Teacher Education*, 27(4), 751–61.

U.S. Department of Education (2016). Federal work study (FWS) program. Retrieved from http://www2.ed.gov/programs/fws/index.html.

Washington State Board for Community and Technical Colleges. (1994). *Best practices: A resource book for volunteer tutoring program coordinators.* Olympia, WA. Retrieved from http://www.eric.ed.gov/contentdelivery/servlet/ERICServlet?accno=ED378383.

Wasik, B. A. (1998). Volunteer tutoring programs in reading: A review. *Reading Research Quarterly*, 33(3), 266–91.

Youth Today. (2016). Youth today: Out of school time literacy. Retrieved from http://youthtoday.org/topic/ost-literacy/.

Index

vocabulary, 84; culture and, 84; ELLs and, 17; instruction and, 68–69; mathematics and, 17–19. *See also* language

Whitehurst, G. J., 6
writing: in classrooms, 69; communication through, 21–22; curriculum for, 80; for

emergent bilinguals, 69–70; mathematics and, 22

Yolen, Jane, 86
Youth Today, 100

About the Editors

Dr. Megan Adams is assistant professor of reading education and codirector of the Center for Literacy and Learning at Kennesaw State University in Kennesaw, Georgia. Adams's passion for teaching began in a rural county working with marginalized youth; her lines of research are related to those students, their stories, and the empowerment of teachers who work with marginalized populations.

After working as a teacher and graduation coach, Adams continued to develop her research and teaching by working in teacher education.

Adams currently teaches primarily in graduate reading programs focused on language and literacy and serves on doctoral committees as a content expert or qualitative methodologist. Her research focuses on the scholarship of teaching and learning.

Adams enjoys spending time with her partner, AJ, and her two children.

Dr. Sanjuana Rodriguez is assistant professor of reading and literacy education and codirector of the Center for Literacy and Learning at Kennesaw State University. Rodriguez began her career as a kindergarten teacher and later became a literacy coach for a school district.

Her research interests include the early literacy development of culturally and linguistically diverse students, early writing development, and literacy development of English Learners. She is also interested in how preservice and in-service teachers can implement a curriculum that meets the needs of diverse learners. She has published in *Language Arts*, *Language Arts Journal of Michigan*, and the *Journal of Language and Literacy Education*.

Dr. Kate Zimmer is assistant professor of special education at Kennesaw State University in Kennesaw, Georgia. Prior to working in higher education, Zimmer worked in elementary schools.

Her teaching, research, and community engagement efforts focus on teacher preparation, early intervention, literacy, and autism. She has coordinated several programs in special education at Kennesaw State and has developed a KSU graduate certificate in autism spectrum disorders. Zimmer currently coordinates efforts to merge literacy, special education, and educational leadership through the CEEDAR (Collaboration for Effective Educator Development, Accountability and Reform) group at Kennesaw State. In her spare time she enjoys spending time with her three sons and her husband.

About the Contributors

Dr. Melissa Driver's first experience working in a school setting was not as a teacher. After graduating from college, she worked with AmeriCorps as a disaster relief volunteer, reopening schools throughout Louisiana after Hurricanes Katrina and Rita. Through this experience she was compelled to enter the teaching profession and became a special educator in a middle school program for students who had been retained at least twice.

In her first year of teaching she assumed the role of the special education school site facilitator; worked collaboratively with general educators, administrators, and parents; struggled tremendously while learning how to teach; and fell in love with advocating for students with disabilities.

Driver's classroom experiences led her to work as an instructional coach, supporting teachers during their first few years with a focus on elementary and special education. After two years coaching teachers, she felt she needed to learn more about evidence-based practices and effective school models. This desire took her to the University of Virginia, where she completed a PhD in special education, and then to Kennesaw State University, where she is an assistant professor. Her research and teaching focuses on teacher preparation and support, particularly in preparing teachers to work with students with disabilities, with culturally and linguistically diverse populations, and in the area of mathematics.

Dr. Joanna Simpson is director of academic programs and associate professor at Grand Canyon University in Phoenix, Arizona. After nearly ten years as an inner-city high school English teacher, Simpson made the move into higher education. She has spent the last several years teaching literacy, gifted education, and doctoral research courses to preservice and continuing teachers. She has extensive experience in writing curriculum for initial certification and advanced degree programs and has served as a director of urban education, reading, and gifted programs.

Simpson has published two books: *Sexual Content in Young Adult Literature: Reading between the Sheets* (2015) and *Understanding Gifted Adolescents: Accepting the Exceptional* (2015), coauthored by Megan Adams. Her areas of research and expertise include gifted education, adolescent literacy, and differentiated instruction with a focus on marginalized populations. When she is not writing, she can be found in her pool with her husband, two children, and dogs.

Dr. Natasha A. Thornton is assistant professor of reading and literacy education at Kennesaw State University in Kennesaw, Georgia. Prior to working in higher education, Thornton was an elementary school teacher and literacy coach.

At Kennesaw State University, Thornton teaches literacy methods courses and is involved in research and various projects that support teacher candidates with developing asset-based beliefs and pedagogies to frame their literacy instruction.

Thornton's research interests include culturally relevant literacy instruction, teacher development, and formative experiment research. She has published in *Journal of Language and Literacy Education, Language Arts*, and *Language Arts Journal of Michigan*. In her spare time she enjoys spending time with her husband and two sons, EJ and Cam.

74727107R00080

Made in the USA
San Bernardino, CA
19 April 2018